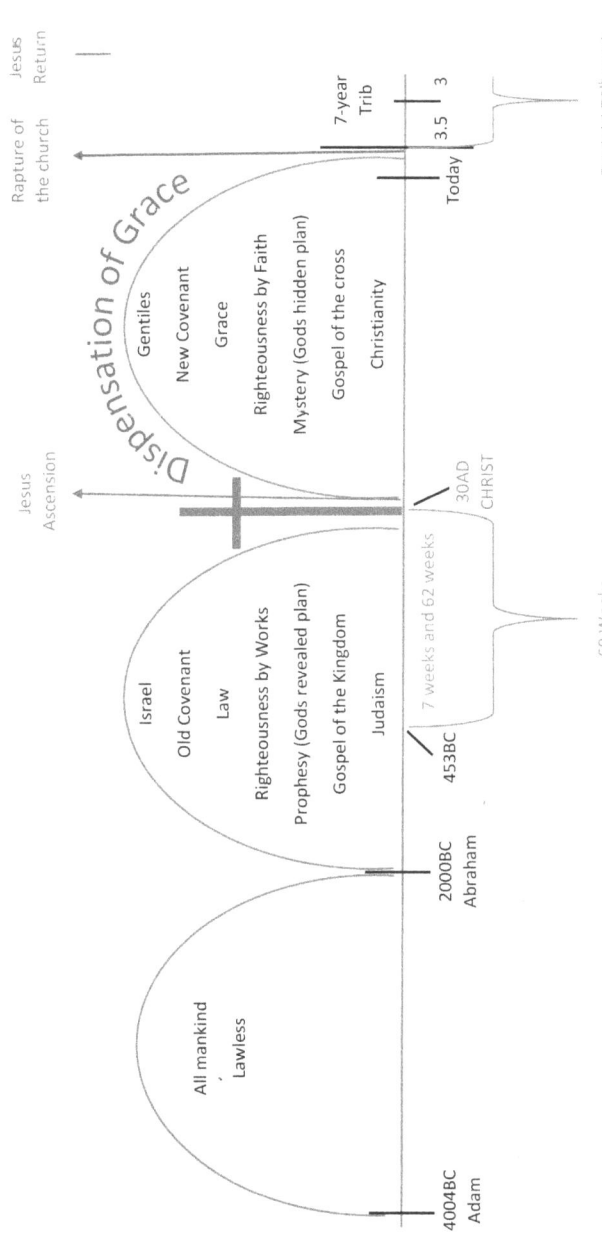

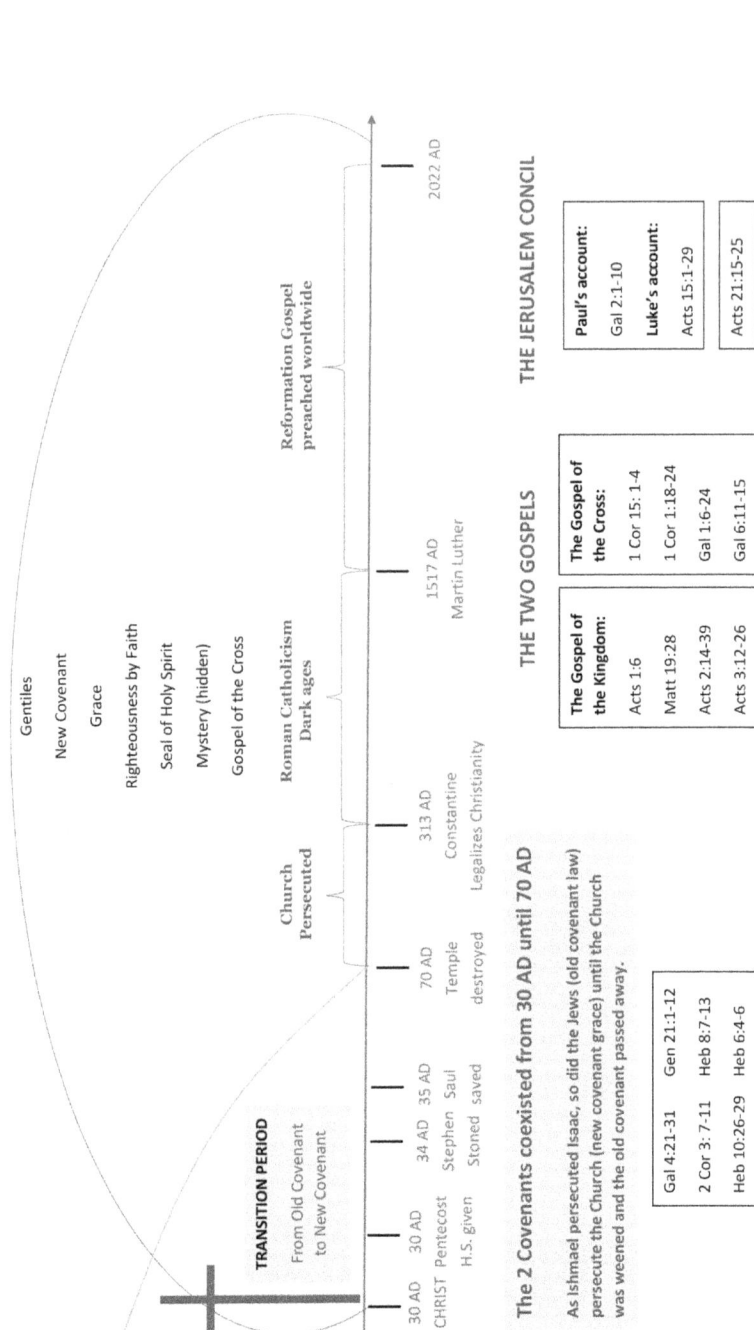

7 FEASTS

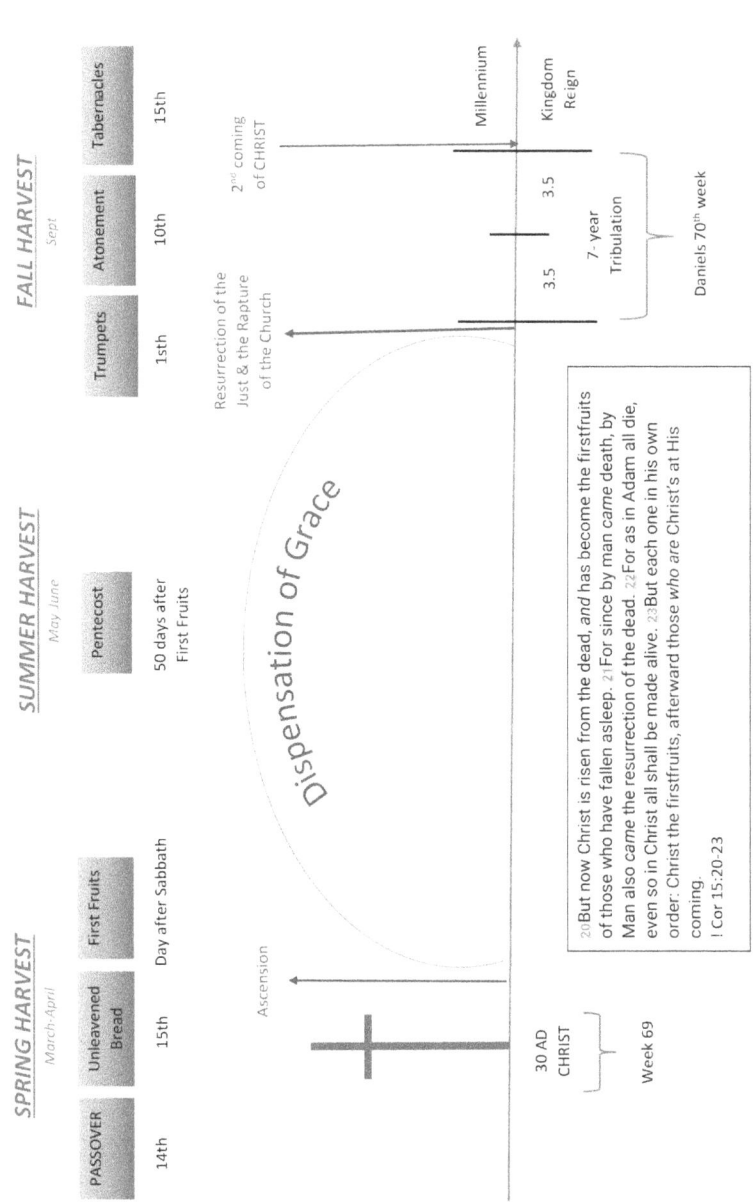

The Plan of God From the Beginning

debi grant

The Plan of God From the Beginning

Permission is granted by the author with proper reference for quotes, to share any portion of this teaching. Jesus Christ said, "Go ye into all the world and preach the gospel to every creature." Mark 16:15

All scripture quoted is from the King James Version

ISBN: 978-1-963611-80-9
LCCN: 2024924654

Cover design: Bob Ousnamer
Cover photo: debi grant

Published by EA Books Publishing, a division of
Living Parables of Central Florida, Inc. a 501c3

EABooksPublishing.com

TABLE OF CONTENTS

Author's Note ix

OLD TESTAMENT
1. In the Beginning 1
2. Lawlessness. 11
3. Age of the Law 19

NEW TESTAMENT
4. Is Jewish 37
5. Age of Grace. 53
6. Saul Becomes Paul 59
7. Seven Feasts Revealed 89
8. Tribulation to New Heaven. 105

A NOTE FROM THE AUTHOR

The Bible has much more for us than this condensed version of nuggets. This will get you started with some background, but I hope you will read the whole Bible. Wisdom comes from knowing the entire Bible and requires the understanding that what was presented was to the Jew until the books of Paul, who learned the reason for the cross from Christ and taught grace to everyone alike.

The words written before the cross are essential examples for every aspect of our lives today. Those inspired words detail what happened to guide and encourage us to a glorious life here. The New Testament verses after the cross urge us to keep our faith for eternity with God after we transition there.

Beginning with Genesis (the word Genesis means "beginning"), I only lay a mini-foundation of biblical events to illustrate the difference between obeying God's voice by works of the Law (obligation) or honoring the grace Jesus gave us from the cross with our free will—God's plan from the beginning.

I hope some of the segments presented here, of people and events from the Word, will be familiar and that I may fit the pieces of your memories together into a sturdy picture of the Bible. The glue of love holds the pieces securely into place so we can endure the jostling and tempest of life.

John 3:16, "For God so loved the world . . . "

Our Father God in heaven has many children—all of us from the past and all of us yet to be born. Like a child looking to a parent to say, "I luv you," all we know of love is what we have experienced. We cannot comprehend the magnitude of love the Trinity has for us.

I hope you begin to understand the meaning of that precious love and let it saturate your being, transforming you into the beacon of light for which you were created, in the image of God, with all His emotions.

This presentation is mostly the result of notes taken over a few years of Sunday school lessons taught by Matthew S. Vila. Added to those notes are my recollections from years of study. Also, by first name, I have mentioned students' relevant comments to Matt's lessons. Their quotes are in {}.

Matt was raised in church but began to doubt his salvation when he compared doctrines of different denominations that contradicted each other. He reread the Bible and prayed throughout. The Spirit gave him direction and clarity. Now, he is sharing his results with us, a class full of believers, at the Tree of Life Church in Naples, Florida;

his classes are ongoing. I have condensed two years of his teaching here for your benefit.

I used to teach children three sessions each Sunday for age groups between five and twelve. Teaching the same lesson three times ingrained the Word into me. I thank God for that. Teaching the very young, the young, and the mid-youth taught me to simplify the Word to the core message. Three years of my life were dedicated to this.

I use the King James Version here, but I've often changed the ye, thou, and thee to you for your ease of reading. Also, I will capitalize the "h" in Him or He when the text is referring to God and replace the "eth" suffix with an "s" when quoting scripture, which changes, for instance, the word eateth to eats. You're welcome. Sometimes, I will note words from the original manuscripts for you when their meanings are especially explanatory.

Let's begin with a prayer. *Dear Heavenly Father, We are so grateful for your Word to guide us through this maze of life. Help us to remember what we read, to feel it, and to sort out Your purpose for our lives. Let our minds understand, and our hearts absorb the measure of Your will for each of us as we read Your Word together. We pray, Amen*

PART ONE

OLD TESTAMENT

CHAPTER ONE

IN THE BEGINNING

Genesis 1:1: "In the beginning . . ." The Hebrew language has three words we translate in English as 'beginning."

One is the ordinal number "first." That was not the Hebrew word used here. Let me explain the third word in Genesis, "In the beginning . . ." with the Hebrew meaning like this: It's a long story of mine to tell. (God has no beginning or end) So, let me just start here as it pertains to you.

> Genesis 1:26: "And God (Elohim "El-oh-heem" in the original Hebrew) said, Let us make man in our image, after our likeness. . . ."

Who is "us"?

Elohim is a plural word in Hebrew meaning Gods, as in the Trinity of God the Father, God the Son and God the Holy Spirit. This Triune (three in one) God has the same objective mind and pureness of heart. It's all about love.

Genesis 1:28–30: "And God blessed them (Adam and Eve), and God said unto them. Be fruitful and multiply and replenish the earth and subdue it. And have dominion over the fish of the sea, and over the fowl of the air, and over every living thing that moves upon the earth. 29 And God said, Behold, I have given you every herb bearing seed, which is upon the face of all the earth, and every tree, in the which is the fruit of a tree yielding seed; to you it shall be for meat. 30 And to every beast of the earth, and to every fowl of the air, and to every thing that creeps upon the earth, wherein there is life, I have given every green herb for meat: and it was so."

Genesis 2:15–17: "And the Lord God took the man and put him into the garden of Eden to dress it and to keep it. 16 And the Lord God commanded the man, saying, Of every tree of the garden thou may freely eat. 17 But of the tree of the knowledge of good and evil, thou shalt not eat of it, for in the day that thou eat thereof thou shalt surely die."

Genesis 2:25: "And they were both naked, the man and his wife, and were not ashamed."

> Genesis 3:6–7 "And when the woman saw that the tree was good for food and that it was pleasant to the eyes, and a tree to be desired to make one wise, she took of the fruit thereof and did eat, and gave also unto her husband with her, and he did eat. 7 And the eyes of them both were opened, and they knew that they were naked, and they sewed fig leaves together and made themselves aprons."

With Adam and Eve's first act of disobedience, sin and the resulting shame entered their lives. Next, they hid from God. (Genesis 3:8) Shame is the emotional response to willful disobedience (sin) to God's Word. After God determined their life's course from this point on, He made a covering for their shame. He made them clothes. For this, the life of an animal had to be sacrificed. (Leviticus 17:11 and Hebrews 9:11).

> Genesis 3:21: "Unto Adam also and to his wife did the Lord God make coats of skins and clothed them."

Imagine how emotionally devastating this was to Eve and Adam. Oh, the regrets! To make atonement is to cover. This began the blood sacrifice to cover human disobedience.

The knowledge of good and evil was passed genetically (we are what we eat) to their offspring. They chose it with their free will, so God honored their choice. The knowledge of evil was allowed to be made known to man.

Everyone still has a choice to do good or not good, but the knowledge of evil was made known to man by a fallen angel.

This angel didn't just fall. He was thrown out of heaven for his pride and a third of heaven's angels went with him as spirits to the earth. They chose.

Heaven was pure and holy once again. And still is.

Now, the war that started in heaven is on earth. What Eve heard came through a snake by a mean spirit that made the snake speak, making fun of God's Word and twisting it into a lie. See Genesis Chapter 3:1–5.

> Genesis 3:4: "And the serpent said to the woman, you shall not surely die. 5 For God knows in the day you eat thereof, then your eyes shall be opened, and you shall be as gods, knowing good and evil."

Did you catch how God's spoken Words were changed to suit an evil purpose? This is one very good reason to read and to know God's Word—so we can rely on it—for our protection against deception.

Adam and Eve did not die physically for many years, but their spiritual covering left them. They died spiritually.

The "dead spirit," or lack of, was passed on to us by Adam. The Good News now is that the eternal Holy Spirit of God is again ours the moment we choose to invite Him to live in our hearts. We will be reborn.

Every day, we decide to feed our soul with the essence of heavenly influence, the words of the Bible, or not to feed ourselves. To meditate (recall these words to mind) and not to entertain thoughts from the lust of our flesh that leads to harmful results.

We have to choose between going by God's written Words, which are written clearly enough to understand, or entertaining thoughts of temptation, those ideas that pop into our minds. By considering those thoughts, the draw of our fleshy nature precludes the next step of planning the wrong deed and preparing for it.

Those ideas come from an outside influence. This fallen angel, now a spirit spitting anger at God, can whisper ideas into our minds, but he cannot read our minds. Only God knows all our thoughts. Big difference!

With a third of heaven's once-angels prowling the earth with their leader in spirit form (invisible to us), we should maybe not talk out loud to ourselves so much. Revelation 12:7–9 lands in the middle of a cryptic message for the end times as an explanation of why Satan is so angry with God and His people. The "war in heaven" happened early in Earth's history, perhaps when Adam and Eve were still new to the Garden, playing with all the animals who only ate grass. Yet, the serpent's anger rages on. Verses 7–9 tell us that Satan, "that old dragon," was cast out of heaven, with a third of the angels who chose his side. He lost that war in heaven and again at the cross, but an end is coming for him. (Revelation 20:10)

Later in Luke, Jesus spoke to His seventy faithful followers,

> Luke 10:18: "And He said unto them, I beheld Satan as lightning fall from heaven."

What are the differences between these two choices of good or evil? Answer: The results of the choice. God's Word is always good for us—full of light and life, great joy and peace.

Yielding to His Holy Spirit, known occasionally in Scripture as "wisdom," produces spiritual fruit, nine of which are described in Galatians 5:22–23, but there are more fruits!

When your mind operates with His Spirit's peace and wisdom, there is no room for anxiety, worry, or fear. Faith is the opposite of fear. It's your choice to make.

To choose any other path is not good for us physically, as the weight of shame and guilt will emotionally drain our health, compounded with the stress of regret.

The malicious one who puts that idea into our mind will not tell us the consequences, only all the fun we will miss if we go to our boring Bible for answers. If we choose the wider path, that demeaning spirit will later ridicule us for our failures. Oh, he will remind us often how we've failed! He will heap regrets onto shame, keeping us knocked down with doubts into depression.

Well, he tries. If we ever learned anything from the Bible, it is, Jesus loves me, this I know. This is not an actual quote. It is the message we receive from reading His Word, and that He will return to lift us. So, hold on.

All sin is committed toward God; it goes against His Word. Even if one person may hurt another by striking, wounding, or even murder, the disobedience is first against God's Word, and He will repay. There will be a judgment day.

He has written His laws onto our hearts and minds. Like any good parent, God warns us first. Our conscience tells us. Our Father gives, maybe with varied amounts of leniency, gives us time to reconsider. However, intentional, blatant disregard for God's Word, made by a determined choice, deserves some consequence. God is good, and God is just. We will not be punished for what we don't know. Rest assured of that.

Adam and Eve gave birth to a son, Cain. He became a tiller of the ground. Then, Able was born. He tended the sheep.

To prepare a sacrifice to God, Cain, the older brother, had to ask his baby brother for a lamb. Soon, Cain got the idea to offer the best of his work, the best of his crop, to God for a sacrifice. Do you wonder where that thought came from? The idea boosted his pride. Pride, by the way, is the root of all evil.

Why wouldn't the best of what Cain brought be a worthy sacrifice? Because that is not what God deemed as a sacrifice. Blood means death. It is why the death of God's only beloved Son is such a big deal.

Adam and Eve experienced the death of a sacrifice to cover their sin firsthand. They told their children what happens when you decide to go against Authority. Abel's sacrifice was accepted, and Cain's was not. Cain was disgruntled about that. Then,

> Genesis 4:8–10: "And Cain talked with Abel his brother; and it came to pass, when they were in the field, that Cain rose up against Abel his brother, and slew him. 9 And the Lord said unto Cain, Where is Abel, thy brother? And he said, I know not: Am I my brother's keeper? 10 And He said, What have you done? The voice of your brother's blood cries unto me from the ground."

See the opportunity for Cain to confess? (verse 9). I don't hear any regret or the shame his parents experienced. Do you? God didn't hear any regret either. No confession of guilt or asking for forgiveness. Cain was banished to another land.

Eve bore another son to Adam. She named him Seth. That name means "appointed," for she said, "God has appointed me another seed . . ." (Genesis 4:25).

No truer words were spoken, as Jesus Christ came from the seed of Seth four thousand years later.

CHAPTER TWO

LAWLESSNESS

The population of the earth grew, mostly into depravity. They did not have the guidance of the Holy Spirit in them. People did what they thought was right for them. The Word of God was handed down by mouth. If only children would listen to their parents and honor their Maker.

In Genesis Chapter 6, the Bible explains how the angels in heaven, "sons of God," (verse 2), can see the people on earth. As angels, they can pass from heaven to earth. (Also described in the dream of Jacob, Genesis 28:10–12). It may be, if they decide to stay, they become like men because angels cannot procreate. (Matthew 22:30). Genesis 6:4 mentions the "giants" and that "the sons of God" did procreate with the "daughters of men" to create "mighty men."

Noah (Genesis chapters 6–11) from the lineage of Seth, pure of blood not tainted with the giant's DNA, was chosen by God as the only holy family that honored God left on earth. (Genesis 6:8)

Noah built the ark where his wife, three sons with their wives, and all the chosen animals were packed into the ark, to survive the great flood, meant to destroy the evil of mankind from off the earth.

Question: Were the wives of Noah's sons genetically pure? Doubtful, or their families would also have been saved. And later, there were giants again on the earth. As, there was a city of giants the spies found when they scoped out the Promised Land.

Of Noah's three sons, Shem (Genesis 11:10) carried the lineage leading to Christ. After Shem, it was about five hundred years to Abraham (Genesis 11:27) who was called out of his pagan nation (Genesis 12:1) to become the first chosen Hebrew, 2000 years after Adam.

Abraham's father was a maker of idols. There were more Gentiles than God-honoring people of this time. Strong but few, God's devoted people were in sparse groups scattered across Canaan. To honor God, many practiced the atonement of an animal sacrifice, mentioned also in Job ("Joe-ba").

NOTE: Scholars consider the story of Job, as happening around the time of Abraham, to be handed down in verbal form until it was recorded in written form. Did Moses write the Book of Job? I think so. Scholars are undecided. They also consider Solomon or Ezra, the priest/scribe, the other best choices. Moses wrote what God told him to write, becoming the first five books of the Bible, called the Torah. Moses may have asked God about the story he had heard. I love the wisdom in Job! Considering the extensive conversations between Job, the four men, and God, I vote for Moses writing what God said. Job teaches us about faithfulness to God when all is in the dumpster and stinky. With all his misery, Job didn't take his own life; he kept his faith. Job is my hero.

As he was called at birth, Abram became Abraham, by God's promise, to be the father of many nations. The promise God gave to Abraham includes this blessing:

> Genesis 12:1–3: "Now the Lord had said unto Abram, Get out of your country and your kindred and from your father's house unto a land that I will show you. 2 And I will make of thee a great nation, I will bless you and make your name great, and you shall be a blessing. 3 And I will bless them that bless you and curse him that curses you, and in thee shall all the families of the earth be blessed."

God's covenant promise concerns a new land and people. Verse 3 is God's promise to Abraham and his seed. So, being adopted into God's family becomes our blessing.

Because this is a covenant promise, God is legally bound to give good or bad in response to the actions of anyone who blesses Abraham's seed or curses them. He is the Rewarder and a just Judge.

That was quite a miraculous promise, considering Abram was 75 when God spoke it. The promise was fulfilled when Abraham was 100 years old and Sarah 90, far past the age of conceiving and giving birth. (Genesis 17:17) Their son, Isaac, promised by God (Genesis 12:4) was the first miraculous birth in Scripture. Giving us a great memory verse,

> Genesis 18:14: "Is any thing too hard for the Lord?"

Actually, Abraham had two sons. The firstborn came when Sarah offered her handmaid to Abraham as a surrogate—about ten years after God promised her husband to be the father of many nations. (Don't we try to help God fix things? This story should cure us of that.) This was common practice of that day. The bondwoman gave birth to Ishmael, Abraham's firstborn, but he was not the child God promised to him. Ishmael went on to have twelve sons that became present-day Turkey, Syria, Pakistan, and Iran, to name a few.

The blessing for the Hebrew nation began with Abraham's second born, Isaac.

> Genesis 17:21 But my covenant will I establish with Isaac, which Sarah shall bear

unto thee at this set time in the next year. (Isaac was named by God before his birth.)

Genesis 17 also declares circumcision as a sign of the Covenant people. Several years later, when God wanted to prove Abraham's faith and trust, God asked him to:

> Genesis 22:2: "And He said, Take now thy son, thine only son Isaac, whom you love, and get into the land of Moriah; and offer him there for a burnt offering upon one of the mountains which I will tell you of."

As great of a challenge as you can imagine, Abraham was faithful, believing God had promised him a nation would flow from Isaac. Who could guess how God was going to perform that with Isaac dead? With faith in God's promise, Abraham went through with it until the raising of the knife, ready to thrust Isaac through, when an angel of God stopped him.

God is all-knowing. That mountain called Moriah became known as Golgotha, the same spot on which Christ was crucified some 2,000 years later.

> John 3:16: "For (Father) God so loved the world, He gave His only begotten Son (Jesus) that whomsoever believes in Him should not perish but have everlasting life."

Abraham's "only" son was soon to multiply into a great nation from Isaac's second born, Jacob. The twelve sons of Jacob, who God renamed "Israel," were called the twelve tribes of Israel as they began to multiply. Who collectively became the nation of Israel, of which Jesus was born, from the tribe of Judah.

Isaac, that first miracle child, was made to wait 20 years after he married Rebekah for her to conceive. She had twin sons! One of the sons was destined to fulfill God's promise. Jacob (means deceiver) swindled the birthright from his older twin, Esau.

Then, under his mother's direction, they stole Esau's Patriarchal blessing. It is hard to believe that Jacob was the chosen one of God.

Jacob had to flee from Esau's rage to his mother's country for the next 20 years. There, he met the girl of his dreams. (Genesis 29). Complicated as life became, he had 12 sons during those 20 years by four women. By the time he returned home, Esau was friendly, and they soon buried their father, Isaac, together. (Genesis 35: 27–29)

The twelve sons of Jacob became the patriarchs of Israel's history, the twelve tribes of Israel, as God changed Jacob's name to Israel (Genesis 32:28). "Abraham, Isaac, and Jacob" is still the mantra of the "Fathers" of Jewish history.

After Jacob's favorite son, Joseph, at age 17 (Genesis 37:2), was sold into slavery by his jealous brothers (Genesis 37:12), he ended up in Egypt, and there arose a famine lasting seven years. Joseph was second only to Pharaoh, in charge of the distribution of corn, making Pharaoh the wealthiest man on earth because Joseph's wisdom came from God (Genesis 41:38–40).

When Joseph met his brothers again, who came to ask for corn, he was soon reunited with all his family. (Genesis 46) Pharaoh gave them the land of Goshen in Egypt when the family was 70 persons strong. As the years passed, the new Pharaoh decided to make slaves of them, as they multiplied so fast. 400 years of slavery followed (Exodus 1:8–11).

CHAPTER THREE

AGE OF THE LAW

The first 2000 years of Adam to Abraham was known as the Age of Lawlessness. People did what they thought was right in their own eyes.

The following years begin the Age of the Law with Moses leading the Hebrew Israelites out of Egypt.

Phenomenal miracles were performed in this endeavor, ending with the parting of the Red Sea to allow the escape of God's people. Then, the closing of the sea when Pharaoh's army tried to pass through.

Following quickly came the Ten Commandments and the laws in the book of Deuteronomy, totaling 613 laws to help this massive group of people behave. The main theme of the laws in Deuteronomy is this from God: If you obey the laws, I will bless you. If you do not obey, expect curses in your life.

The Old Testament's Twelve tribes of Israel were called by God "His chosen people." They are considered His children, heirs of the Father God.

A few details . . .

By the time Moses was born (Exodus Chapter 2) and began to deliver the slaves out of Egypt, they were about two million strong. Moses was 80 years old when God plagued Egypt with ten plagues, one for each of their false gods. The Hebrews did not suffer the effects of the last seven plagues, even when a darkness so thick it could be felt plagued Egypt for three days.

Most importantly, the last one (Exodus 11) meant death to the firstborn, of man and beast.

Almighty God instituted a meal for the Hebrews to observe that night of a whole lamb, slain with no bones broken. Using its blood to mark the lintel and doorposts so the death angel could see the blood and would pass over them. The meal was named "Passover," and the tradition is still celebrated today. Many details are significant to God's firstborn, Jesus, the holy Lamb of God (Exodus 12:1–13, 21–30).

> Exodus 12:14: "And this day shall be unto you for a memorial, and you shall keep it a feast to the Lord throughout your generations, you shall keep it a feast by an ordinance forever."

Pharaoh insisted the Hebrew slaves and their families leave Egypt after that night. 430 years since the day they entered Egypt as a people (Exodus 13:40).

NOTE: It just so happens that at the end of the Old Testament is the prophetic book of Malachi. Then, there were 400 years of silence with no prophet to speak to God's people until the birth of Christ. The age of Jesus, old enough to begin His Priesthood, according to the law, was age 30 (400 + 30). He was crucified 3 years later (with no bones broken) and set us free. (Joseph was in Egypt about three years before his brothers came. Two were spent in prison.)

After leaving Egypt, God moved mightily in the lives of the freed Hebrews with miracle after wondrous miracles throughout their journey of 40 years—for an eleven-day trip to the Jordan River. Sadly, the people were not receptive to trusting in the Mighty God of Moses, even after those ten plagues and the Red Sea miracle. It was their unbelief that God would protect and provide for them; that unbelief held them back from their Promised Land.

They feared God with the fear of a wild beast, not with the reverential fear they needed to feel honored, blessed, protected, and provided for, although our Holy God did all those things. They complained all their days and wallowed in worry and unbelief. (Hint for us).

Except for the sin sacrifice. They did believe they could transfer their sin by laying their hand on the head of an innocent lamb, bull, or goat to atone for their sin. Because of their lack of trust, Moses was not able to deliver the Hebrews into the land promised by God to Abraham. They walked around the desert and Mt. Sinai until all their generation died. They lived in tents to make moving easy, following the pillar of cloud by day (it gave them shade) or the pillar of fire by night (for heat). Scripture calls them His peculiar people (Exodus 19:5).

When Moses was about to die, God blessed Joshua to take over for Moses. Joshua led the second generation of Hebrews over the Jordan River with Caleb, the only other survivor from the first generation. Both survived because of their firm belief in God. They were the only two who believed God would prevail in their conquest of the giants in the Promise Land. All the others wished they were back in Egypt.

Here is how God encouraged Joshua. (Joshua 1:5–9).

> Joshua 1:5–6 "There shall not any man be able to stand before you all the days of thy life; as I was with Moses, so I will be with you. I will not fail thee, nor forsake thee. 6) Be strong and of a good courage . . . "

> Joshua 1:9: "Have not I commanded you? Be strong and of a good courage, be not afraid, neither be dismayed, (doubt, wonder, worry) for the Lord thy God is with you, where ever you go."

Joshua was such a strong believer that he asked God for the sun to stand still—out loud—in front of everyone who could hear—until he finished fighting the enemy. See Joshua Chapter 10.

Israel's hero, David, who slew the giant Goliath, is included in this Age of the Law, all the way to the death of Christ about 33 AD. There are only two people groups now, the Gentiles and the Israelites (Hebrews/Jews).

Of the Israelites, only the Levites, from the tribe of Levi, were entrusted with the scrolls of the Law, the scrolls of the prophets, and the Psalms. The Levite Priests taught the other tribes.

Some of their servants and other Gentiles were allowed to listen to the Word with them. Isaiah 60:3 tells us that Israel's purpose is to be a light to the Gentiles, who could be converted and adopted as Jews if they confessed their belief in Almighty Jehovah (God's name), became circumcised, and promised to follow the laws.

Which nobody could ever do, hard as they tried. God called David to be king of Israel at age seven and was anointed King by the prophet Samuel. Then, David went back to caring for his father's sheep. Saul, from the tribe of Benjamin, was the current king and continued to sit on the throne for many years, but the favor of God and His Spirit had left Saul because he was disobedient to the prophet Samuel.

David loved God more than anything. He was so angry at Goliath for insulting God that he was determined to kill him, convinced God would aid him in the slaying. David slew Goliath (I Samuel 17) at about age 14 and won the hearts of Israel's people.

King Saul asked David to join him as his son-in-law and eat at the king's table. Soon, a jealous rage stirred up in Saul's heart, and he began to pursue David, trying to kill him.

Wisdom was given to David at every turn, as God's favor was on him. Men came from all over, by the hundreds, to join and protect David on his quest to hide from Saul and the army of Israel. David covered much ground during his ten-plus years quest to stay clear of Saul. He carried himself wisely, acted fairly (in those days' terms), and gained an honorable reputation among all the lands.

Saul was sorely wounded in battle with the Philistines. He went aside in his chariot, then "fell on his sword" to keep from being abused by the enemy. Three of his sons died in the long days' battle with him. The king was dead.

All of Judah wanted David to become king to replace Saul. (II Samuel 2) David, age 30, brought his wives and his "mighty men" with him to be anointed by the people and reigned in Hebron for seven years and six months.

While another of Saul's sons, Ishbosheth reigned over Israel's remaining tribes until his death by treason. David not only lamented Saul's death and his sons, but he also mourned the murder of Ishbosheth. Speaking to the one who brought the head of Saul's son to him, David said:

> II Samuel 4:10–11 "When one told me, saying, Behold, Saul is dead, thinking to have brought good tidings, I took hold of him, and slew him in Ziklag, who thought that I would have given him a reward for his tidings 11 How much more, when wicked men have slain a righteous person (Ishbosheth) in his own house upon his bed? Shall I not therefore now require his blood of your hand, and take you away from the earth?"

And that he did. All the elders of the tribes of Israel came to Hebron to ask David to reign over all the tribes of Israel. They reminded him of how he led the people after slaying Goliath.

They loved him, saying they were family (II Samuel 5:1) "Thy bone and thy flesh." After he and his army conquered the Jebusites of Jerusalem, David called it Zion and reigned over all 12 tribes of Israel from Jerusalem for the next 33 years, building it up. He took out all the opposing nations with a mighty army, making some of the captives servants, hewers of wood, and water bearers. He made treaties with other nations, to bring tribute to Jerusalem, from the necessities of corn, barley, flour, oil, timber to silver and gold, which he laid up in store.

He made harps and other instruments for the sons of Levi to worship the Lord. David wanted to build God a house for the Ark of the Covenant, the holy place where the Ten Commandments were kept. This golden ark was topped by the mercy seat, where God, in Spirit, could be spoken to. At that time, the ark was under a tent since the days of Moses, when it was called "the tent of meeting."

With God speaking through the prophet, Nathan, a man close to David's heart, Nathan told him, no, yet his son may build God a house (II Samuel 7:1–17),

> Verse 13, "He shall build a house for My name, and I will establish the throne of his kingdom forever."

Prompting such humility and gratefulness in David's heart, he prayed a thankful prayer. Verses 18–29, beginning, "Who am I, O Lord God?" and verse 22, "Wherefore Thou art great, O Lord God; for there is none like Thee, neither is there any God beside Thee, according to all that we have heard with our ears."

The respect David gives to God is awe-inspiring. He wrote most of the Psalms, meant to be put to music and sung as praise to the Wonderful and Almighty God. Many of them prophesy about the coming Messiah and describe the death of Christ, who quoted Psalms from the cross. Some of David's Psalms include clues about end-time events, as well. We could say he was a prophet.

After 40 years as reigning king, David passed the throne to Solomon just before his death. Every king had to be anointed by a prophet. That is why the ruse to make himself king did not work for another of David's sons. Adonijah called many people to celebrate his kingship but was not called or anointed by a prophet. Solomon was given that honor by Nathan, the prophet.

We don't know how old Solomon was (maybe 9–12) when he was anointed King. We read that, "he was tender." His father made provisions to build the temple by collecting gold, silver, precious stones, brass, and timber. David asked the heads of the families because David was old and ready to go to his Father, to help Solomon in this magnificent quest of building and to supply as they desired. They desired much.

Shortly after Solomon was made King, he had a dream-vision where God asked Solomon what He could do for him (I Kings 3:5–15).

> I Kings 3:7–14: "And now, O Lord my God, You have made Thy servant king instead of David my father, and I am but a little child. I know not how to go out or come in. 8 And Thy servant is in the midst of Thy people which You have chosen a great people, that cannot be numbered nor counted for multitude. 9 Give therefore Thy servant an understanding heart to judge Thy people, that I may discern between good and bad, for who is able to judge this, Your so great a people? 10 And the speech pleased the Lord, that

Solomon had asked this thing. 11 And God said unto him, Because you have asked this thing, and have not asked for thyself long life; neither have asked riches...nor...the life of your enemies but have asked for thyself understanding to discern judgment, 12 Behold, I have done according to your words, Lo, I have given you a wise and an understanding heart, so that there was none like before you, neither after you shall any arise like unto thee. 13 And I have also given you that which you have not asked; both riches and honor, so that there shall not be any among the kings like unto you, all thy days. 14 And if you will walk in my ways, to keep my statutes and my commandments, as your father David did walk, then I will lengthen thy days."

When Solomon awoke, he saw it was a dream. He came to Jerusalem to stand before the Ark of the Covenant, offer burnt offerings and peace offerings, and make a feast for all his servants.

Solomon was indeed the most wise person on earth. Kings of other nations came to him for guidance, always bringing gifts. The Queen of Sheba came with a train of camels loaded with a multitude of gifts, and came with some hard questions (I Kings 10:1–10). She didn't go away empty-handed, for those who bless Israel will be blessed.

> I Kings 10:13: "And king Solomon gave unto the queen of Sheba all her desire, whatsoever she asked, beside that which Solomon gave her of his royal bounty. So, she turned and went to her own country, she and her servants."

Remember the promise God made to Abraham? Genesis 12:3 "I will bless them that bless you and curse them that curse you . . ." The rule may have begun with Abraham, but it continues today and will tomorrow. God is still God. He doesn't change, and neither do the Words of His promises. He loves a cheerful giver and blesses you in return.

There was peace throughout Solomon's reign because his father, David, subdued all opposing kingdoms or eradicated them. Those remaining paid tribute to Solomon. In I Kings 10 14–27 describes the wealth coming into the kingdom.

> I Kings 10:14: "Now the weight of gold that came to Solomon in one year was six hundred threescore and six talents of gold. (666) . . . and merchant ships brought spice . . . 18 . . . the king made a great throne of ivory and overlaid it with the best gold . . . 21 . . . all (his) drinking vessels were of gold . . . none were of silver; it was nothing

> accounted of in the days of Solomon . . . 23 So King Solomon exceeded all the kings of the earth for riches and for wisdom. 24 And all the earth sought to Solomon to hear his wisdom, which God had put in his heart. 25 And they brought every man his present, vessels of silver and vessels of gold and garments and armor and spices, horses and mules, a rate year by year . . . 27 And the king made silver to be in Jerusalem as stones . . . "

Being so wise, Solomon wrote (most of) the book of proverbs, simple phrases to teach us wisdom. Also, the book of Ecclesiastes encourages our right to be joyful, and the Song of Solomon shows the love of God for His beloved (that's us).

Not all of Solomon's life was dedicated to the God he so strongly served in the beginning. The lust for women got the better of him. He had over 700 wives and 300 concubines, so he worshiped and sacrificed to their gods, breaking the first commandment."

So, God's promise to David that someone from his seed would continually serve as king remained true, but they did not have all twelve tribes. The kingdom was "rent" after Solomon. Torn. His son ruled over Judah in Jerusalem, with only the tribes of Benjamin and Judah. The other ten tribes were known as Israel, to the north, with a different king.

God Almighty did not divide the kingdom of Solomon in his day because whatever the son does reflects the Father. A son is to be the expressed image of their father. Males introduced themselves as "David, son of Jesse." For example, Ham's son was cursed because Ham saw the nakedness of Noah, his father. God would not soil the reputation of Noah. Nor the reputation of David.

Neither of the divided kingdoms served God continuously, from one king to the next. Most kingdoms did not, with many idols to choose from among the Gentiles living around them and with them, complete with superstitions and ceremonies.

Injustice grieved God. He warned those disobedient, with the voice of many prophets, to care for the fatherless, the poor and needy, the widows and orphans.

The people sacrificed their babies in a fire pit carved into the belly of one of their idols, enraging God.

There were some exceptionally good kings, however. Those who honored and served Him stayed the wrath of God from the disobedient others for a time. However merciful, there was a limit to God's patience when His warnings went unheeded, spoken by many prophets over hundreds of years to people who refused to listen.. Finally, He ended the lives of His chosen people by famine, pestilence, and the sword.

Both Israel and Judah were ravaged by war from many countries, each taking some plunder and captives. Among the early captives were Daniel and his three friends. By

435 BC, the Babylonians finished the siege and carried off the few thousand remaining as captives to Babylon.

Truly, the end of the era, as Solomon's exquisite gold-covered temple was burned with everything in the city, and the Jerusalem's walls were knocked down. There was nothing left.

To summarize God's sentence of wrath on His chosen people, He determined 70 weeks (meaning 70 years in captivity), with no mention of idol worship or the sacrifice of children He abhorred. He said only, from lack of observing the seventh-year Sabbath rest required by the land. There was to be no planting or harvest that seventh year. What may come up on its own was to be used by the poor, not by the landowners. They could plant in the eighth year and reap the end harvest. Until then, Our Almighty Provider would have given such a bountiful crop in the sixth year to carry them until the harvest on the eighth. God keeps His promises, but they didn't do their part.

Jeremiah prophesied this siege of Jerusalem, the savage takeover of Judah by the Babylonians, and he mourned it after the fact in his book of Lamentations.

Even with the banishment of Israel and Judah into slavery, God saved a remnant of His people and made a miraculous way for them to return by prophesying a king 400 years before the event, by name. King Cyrus sent the Jews back home as soon as he became King and funded their journey. They rebuilt a temple and later rebuilt the wall around Jerusalem with the funding of the next Kings, Darius and Artaxerxes.

All a part of God's plan. (See the books of Ezra and Nehemiah) Before these events, the prophet Zechariah writes 8:1–15, the voice of a happy God, declares how wonderful it will be.

> Zechariah 8:5: "And the streets of the city shall be full of boys and girls playing in the streets thereof. 7 Behold, I will save my people from the east country and from the west country, 8 and I will bring them, and they shall dwell in the midst of Jerusalem; and they shall be my people and I will be their God, in truth and in righteousness."

NOTE: King David was from the tribe of Judah, 14 generations after Abraham. From David until the carrying away captive to Babylon, it was 14 generations. From there, it was 14 generations until Jesus was born (Matthew 1:17).

The remaining books of the Old Testament are from the prophets, who are called the major prophets and the minor ones by their length. They each speak wisdom, whether long or short. Isaiah has 66 chapters, often compared to the total of the Bible's 66 books.

Ezekiel and Daniel are the prophets with the most verses concerning end-time prophecies. At our Rapture and Tribulation discussions, we will uncover Daniel's vision concerning the 70 weeks prophesied in Jeremiah and hear from Ezekiel.

PART TWO

NEW TESTAMENT

CHAPTER FOUR

JESUS IS JEWISH

Jesus was born Jewish, from the tribe of Judah, by both Mary's genealogy and His stepfather, Joseph.

But first, Mary's older cousin, Elizabeth, had the honor of another of Scripture's miracle conceptions, giving birth to John, who received the Holy Spirit while in the womb. An angel had told his father, a Levitical priest, that John would tell the world of the coming Messiah. John grew up and, like Paul, got his education in the desert. (See Luke 1:5–2:20, 3:2–22) He began to preach when he turned 30, the age a man could become a priest, saying, "Repent, the kingdom is at hand!"

John, a priest by heritage, did not serve in the synagogue like his father. He served the multitudes of common people, baptizing them in the wilderness of Judea as a prophet, proclaiming the soon coming of the long-awaited Messiah.

Jesus was baptized by "John, the Baptist," as he was called, in the river, Jordan. That act of baptism became

Christ's anointing by the prophet John, technically declaring Jesus the King of the Jews. However, His kingship was not acknowledged until Pilot interviewed Him just before His crucifixion.

Spoken to John by God as a sign to discover the Messiah in the water of the Jordan river (John 1:31–34), the Holy Spirit descended from heaven with the image of a dove onto Him, and the voice of God the Father established Jesus as, "My Beloved Son."

This event, at the age of thirty, began His three-year ministry. Jesus would speak often of the Kingdom that was promised to the Jews throughout the Old Testament. In Nazareth, where He was raised, Jesus read from the scrolls on Sabbath, the appointed reading for that day.

> Luke 4:18–19 (quoting from Isaiah 61:1–2) "The Spirit of the Lord is upon me, because He has anointed me to preach the gospel to the poor; He has sent me to heal the brokenhearted, to preach deliverance to the captives and recovering of sight to the blind, to set at liberty them that are bruised, 19 To preach the acceptable year of the Lord . . . "

Jesus stopped short of reading the last part of verse 2, about "the day of vengeance" written in Isaiah 61. That was not a part of His ministry this time around. It will come after the tribulation, prophesied as Daniel's 70th week. It has waited over 2000 years so far to show itself.

The portion of Isaiah He did read was His appointed mission, certainly fulfilling each phrase. He taught the multitudes and healed all who came to Him. His teachings were intended for the Jew. Paul said,

> Romans 15:8: "Now I say that Jesus Christ was a minister of the circumcision (Jews) for the truth of God, to confirm the promises made unto the fathers. (Abraham, Isaac and Jacob)."

Still, Jesus had an obligation to keep the Covenant Promise made to Abraham, blessing those who bless Israel. He did heal the centurion's servant, as recorded in Luke 7:2–10. The believing elders of the Jews told Christ that this Gentile had built them a synagogue. Not only did Jesus heal the servant, but He did it also from a distance, as the centurion understood the authority of the Lord and knew He could. "Just say the Word," the centurion said. Jesus marveled at that kind of faith!

The strong faith of the Jewish people could have brought all nations to God, as it was mentioned in the Old Testament (Zechariah 8:20–23). Instead, this prophecy will be fulfilled at the end of the tribulation.

> Zechariah 8:23: "Thus says the Lord of hosts; In those days, ten men . . . of (other) languages . . . shall take hold of the skirt of . . . a Jew, saying, we will go with you, for we have heard God is with you."

If only the Jewish leaders of that day would have believed Jesus to be the Messiah! They expected their Messiah to be born in Bethlehem, a sure sign from the prophet Micah.

> Micah 5:2: "But thou, Bethlehem Ephratah, thou be little among the thousands of Judah, Out of thee shall He come forth unto me to be ruler in Israel, Whose goings forth have been from of old, from everlasting."

Jesus never admitted to being born in Bethlehem. King Herod had all the babies killed up to two years of age when the "wise men from the east" didn't return to tell Herod where they found the babe, born King of the Jews. Jesus was spared because an angel warned Joseph in a dream to flee to Egypt with the young child (Matthew 2:1–18).

The Pharisees only knew He was raised in Nazareth. He allowed them to assume He was born there.

> Zechariah 9:9: "Rejoice greatly, O daughter of Zion; Shout, O daughter of Jerusalem:

> Behold, thy King comes unto you, He is just and having salvation; Lowly, and riding upon a donkey, And upon a colt the foal of a donkey."

Jesus fulfilled this prophecy perfectly on the exact day told in Scripture the Messiah would enter Jerusalem.

By not acknowledging Jesus as the Messiah, the Sanhedrim (high council of the Jewish religion) rejected His deity as the Son of Father God. Then, at the stoning of Stephan, after the cross (Acts 6:5–8:4), the Sanhedrin rejected the Holy Spirit, as they clearly saw in Stephen.

> Acts 6:15: "And all that sat in the council looking steadfastly on him, saw his face as it had been the face of an angel."

Had they acknowledged and repented with Stephen instead of blaspheming the Holy Spirit by stoning him to death, the 70th week would have come to pass then. So, the 70th week of Daniel's vision was reduced to fulfilling 69 weeks, with the birth and death of Christ. The 70th week will happen in the future when the "fullness of the Gentiles" has come in. This means until the Gospel is preached to every tongue, tribe, and nation {Ruby: When you witness to someone, you won't realize the chain of events that proceed from your preaching, until you get to heaven}.

> Romans 11:25 ... blindness partly happened for Israel until the fullness of the Gentiles shall come in.

Jesus fulfilled all the writings of the law and all the prophecies about His coming. Never, did He preach the cross. It had not happened yet. There were no Christians before the cross. All the disciples and Jesus were practicing Jews.

Jesus did show the love of His Father God, by displaying great mercy and love for all of creation. So many miracles, healings and raising Lazarus back to a living body after four days in a tomb, no one else had ever done.

He said, if you have seen me, you have seen the Father. He came to show the love of the Father, to save us and heal us with His sacrificial death. This kindness, too, was not what the head council expected from the Messiah. They wanted their King to be a warrior like David, to conquer Roman oppression and restore the Kingdom as was in Solomon's day.

The appearance of Christ as a warrior, Lord of Lords, is prophesied, but those verses are for the end times, to end the Tribulation. Then, Jesus will gather the remnant of His people for the Millennium Reign of peace, with Satan bound in a chain below ground.

Christ had a meal with His disciples the evening He was taken into custody. Often, we refer to this meal as The Last Supper, or a Passover meal, although only bread and oil are mentioned. Unleavened bread portrays Jesus because He was without sin. He even said,

> John 6:35: "I am the bread of life. He that comes to me shall never hunger, and he that believes in me shall never thirst."

> John 6:48, 50–51: "I am that bread of life. 50 This is the bread which comes down from heaven, that a man may eat thereof and not die. 51 I am the living bread which came down from heaven. If any man eat of this bread, he shall live forever and the bread that I will give is my flesh, which I will give for the life of the world."

And at the Last Supper, which we call Communion, He gave unleavened bread to His disciples and declared that it was His (sinless) body.

> Luke 22:19–20: "And he took bread and gave thanks and broke it and gave unto them saying, This is my body which is given for you, this do in remembrance of me. 20 This cup is the new testament in my blood which is shed for you."

May I repeat verse 20? "... the new testament in my blood..." This is rightly where the New Testament begins when Jesus shed His blood for us.

As believers, we are without sin because He paid for it. It's gone. Forgiven. His last words from the cross were, "It is finished."

A "teaching Seder" the evening before Passover, was a common event of that day, for the children to learn the custom, as instructed in Exodus. It is a complicated feast. This well-needed training time is considered a jovial family time. The next evening's Passover Seder would be a dinner attended by family, friends and neighbors, with a children's table set off to the side.

Sound familiar? As Christians, we celebrate Christmas Eve. We also celebrate the season, with month-long events more numerous as the day appears. Each is called a Christmas party, no matter what day it occurs.

The Passover season begins with the selecting of the lamb 5 days before the official Passover meal.

Coming together with His disciples to teach them what they needed to know for the events coming quickly, He washed their feet, even the feet of Judas, before sharing the piece of bread He dipped in sop before dismissing him. John 13:21–31.

> John 13:27: "And after the sop Satan entered into him (Judas). Then said Jesus into him, That thou doest, do quickly."

The rest of the disciples went with Him to the Garden of Gethsemane, singing a hymn along the way. He prayed to the Father for their safety and spoke to them with many words too deep for them to comprehend. He knew He was at the end of His journey, telling them only that He was going away. He wanted to tell His chosen what His death would accomplish.

> John 12:31–32: "Now is the judgment of this world: (for the Jews would not claim Him as Messiah) now shall the prince of this world (Satan) be cast out 32 And I, if I be lifted up from the earth, (hung on the cross) will draw all men unto me."

> John 13:36: "Where I go, you cannot follow me now, but you shall follow me, afterward."

His death was a secret! The secret known only by the Trinity. Not even the angels knew. The secret was to be held from Satan, who would never have encouraged the crucifixion to take place had he known it would be the day of his defeat! Satan wanted Jesus dead before the crowd made Him King.

Matthew Vila, not usually animated when he speaks, got emotional with this one. Can you imagine the angels in heaven drawing their swords as they see Jesus being beaten? They are just waiting for Father to give the signal.

Waiting . . . they are ready to rush to His defense! Then, Christ is led to Golgotha. Waiting . . . what? Nailed to the cross? They didn't know the secret. Christ dies, and God laughs!

> Psalm 2:4: "He (Father God) that sits in the heavens shall laugh. The Lord shall have them in derision." (scornful laughter-ha, HA! Fooled you, devil. Satan has been defeated!)

That's probably when the Father explained it to the heavenly host. Jesus just paid the sin debt! Not only that, but He took away the shame that comes with it. Jesus paved the way to healing our sicknesses and diseases, too!

Having the same mind and heart as Father God and His Holy Spirit, Jesus, the beloved Son, loves us unconditionally, too. More than enough to take the nails from the children He made, who hung Him on the cross from those nails.

> John 3:16: "For God so loved the world, He gave His only begotten Son that whomsoever believes in Him should not perish but have everlasting life."

While fighting for each breath in pain, He prayed to the Father, asking Him to forgive them because they didn't understand what they were doing (Luke 23:34). Jesus knew what He was doing.

He bled out, after six tortuous hours, and died for our disobedience, as the Lamb of God, who took away the sins of the world by sacrificing His innocent life for ours. Unfathomable love!

Jesus did this for us to spend eternity with Them. So, we believers could be blameless in the sight of God, exchanging our disobedience for His right standing with the Father.

> I Peter 1:18–21: We are redeemed . . . 19 ". . . with the precious blood of Christ, as of a lamb without blemish and without spot: 20 Who verily (truthfully) was foreordained before the foundation of the world but was manifest in these last times for you. 21 Who by Him (Jesus) do believe in (Father) God, that raised Him up from the dead, and gave Him glory; that your faith and hope might be in God."

When Jesus died, His Spirit was free to roam. Scripture tells us Jesus went into hell.

> Psalm 16:10: "For Thou will not leave My soul in hell, Neither will You suffer Your Holy One to see corruption (decay)."

48 • THE PLAN OF GOD

> I Peter 3:18–20 "For Christ also has once suffered for sins, the just for the unjust, that he might bring us to God, being put to death in the flesh, but quickened by the Spirit. 19 By which also He went (in spirit—His body still in the tomb, yet not seeing corruption as it says in Psalms) and preached unto the spirits in prison (hell). 20 Which sometime were disobedient, (for example) when once the longsuffering of God waited in the days of Noah . . ."

Jesus went to hell to explain His divinity to all who died before He came to earth as a human. And John the Baptist may have gone before Him to prepare the way! Imprisoned by Herod, John began to suffer despair and doubt. He sent his disciples to question Jesus if He was, indeed, the Messiah. John was beheaded before the cross. You know John was not the silent type. He would still be preaching the coming of the Messiah.

Judas died before the crucifixion happened. He couldn't live with himself after coming to his senses, realizing what he had done in handing over Jesus to the authorities.

Can you imagine how many souls in hell believed Jesus was, in fact, the Messiah and were saved from their presumed end-time judgment? All those who passed since Adam, from the beginning of life on earth, 4,000 years before Christ, now had the chance to believe.

Matt imagines what Christ may have said to them, "Remember that lamb you sacrificed for your sins every time? That was me. That's what I just did."

Their spirits may have risen to heaven at that point, creating a huge vacancy in hell.

Take that, Satan!

We believe that Christ's obedience to the divine plan, to go through the cross, gave us the same righteousness He has with Father God. We have His Holy Spirit in us to guide our decisions and give us the power to overcome temptation. Being full of love for Jesus, how could we sin?

Let me explain the three days and nights in the earth from the Jewish perspective. Genesis 1:15 begins the details of the creation of the heaven and the earth.

> Genesis 1:5: "And God called the light Day and the darkness He called Night. And the evening and the morning were the first day."

Given that the evening is mentioned before the morning in verse 5, the Jews have always acknowledged a day beginning with sundown and ending with sundown for the next day to begin. Also, any bit of time on either side of the sun setting is considered part of that day and is counted as the day.

Arrested in the Garden, His interrogation ran through the night. Appearing before the crowd in the morning, He was then beaten and hung on the cross by 9 AM. The blood lost during the scourging allowed Him to bleed out six hours later, marking 3 PM, the hour the lamb was to be sacrificed for that evening's Passover Seder, as His time of death.

> John 19: 38–42: "And after this Joseph of Arimathea being a disciple of Jesus, but secretly for fear of the Jews, besought Pilate that he might take away the body of Jesus and Pilate gave him leave. He came therefore and took the body of Jesus. 39 And there came also Nicodemus, which at the first came to Jesus by night and brought a mixture of myrrh and aloes, about a hundred-pound weight. 40 Then took they the body of Jesus down, wound it in linen clothes with the spices, as the manner of the Jews is to bury. 41 Now in the place where He was crucified there was a garden, and in the garden a new sepulchre wherein was never a man yet laid. 42 There laid they Jesus, therefore, because of the Jews' preparation day, for the sepulchre was nigh at hand."

Several other scriptures note this occasion and timing before the beginning of the Passover Sabbath:

> Mark 14:1–2 the chief priests decide to put Jesus to death but not on the feast day.

> John 18:28: The Jews did not go in with Jesus to the Judgment Hall when Pilot spoke with Jesus, as that place of a Gentile would defile them for the Passover Sabbath.
>
> Luke 23:16–17: Pilot's words to the crowd, releasing a prisoner for the holiday.
>
> Luke 23:52 Joseph begged the body of Jesus to bury 54 on preparation day before the Sabbath. 55 women saw where He was laid, 56 went home, prepared spices for after the Sabbath to anoint Him.

We see that Jesus died and was put into the sepulchre before sundown. This marks day one. as that portion of a day counts in Jewish tradition. At sundown began the Passover Sabbath, day two. Then, according to Leviticus 23:5–7:

> Leviticus 23:5: "In the fourteenth day of the first month at even(ing) is the Lord's Passover. 6 And on the fifteenth day of the same month is the feast of unleavened bread unto the Lord; seven days you must eat unleavened bread. 7 In the first day you shall have a holy convocation (Sabbath) you shall do no servile work therein."

Two Sabbaths in a row. The 14th day is Passover, and the 15th is a Sabbath rest to begin a week of unleavened bread (actually, 8 days of unleavened bread, as the Passover is also a feast with unleavened bread. They were to have no leaven in their homes during these 8 days). So, the 15th day is our day three for Jesus in the tomb.

> Matthew 28:1: "In the end of the (2nd) Sabbath, as it began to dawn toward the first day of the week, came Mary Magdalene and the other Mary to see the sepulchre."

Although the second Sabbath would have ended at sundown, and day four began, there is no way the women would approach the area of the tombs at night. Robbers and thieves were known to hang out there after dark. It was not acceptable for the women and would not have been safe. Verse 1 in Matthew 28 above is in the early morning hours of daylight on the 16th day of the month, day four, and the tomb was empty!

NOTE: Scholars and theologians agree this day is the anniversary of the day the Ark of Noah touched the ground.

CHAPTER FIVE

THE AGE OF GRACE

Returning from hell to earth, Jesus rose from the grave in His glorified body, alive and victorious! His resurrection means Father God accepted His blood sacrifice. Jesus conquered death, freed the captives of hell, and accomplished new life for us, too, with His first resurrected body. The prophets coming out of their graves contribute to that acknowledgment.

Luke writes that three women came to find the empty tomb. They tried to tell the disciples. Most didn't believe them.

> Luke 24:11–12: "And their words seemed to them (the disciples) as idle tales, and they believed them not. 12 Then arose Peter and ran unto the sepulchre, and stooping down, he beheld the linen clothes laid by themselves, and departed, wondering in himself at that which was come to pass."

John 20:4–10 (testament of the Beloved John, "the other disciple" after Mary Magdalene came to tell the disciples of the empty tomb) "So they (Peter and John) ran both together and the other disciple did outrun Peter and came first to the sepulchre. 5 And he stooping down, saw the linen clothes lying; yet went he not in. 6 Then came Simon Peter following him, and went into the sepulchre and sees the linen clothes lie, 7 And the napkin, that was about His head, not lying with the linen clothes, but wrapped together in a place by itself. 8 Then went in also that other disciple . . . and he saw and believed. 9 For as yet they knew not the scripture, that He must rise again from the dead."

From verse 7, the folded napkin above is taught by Messianic Jews (those who believe in Jesus as the Messiah) to signify Jesus's coming back. When a Jew leaves the dinner table for a moment, he folds his napkin so the servants don't clear his plate. He is returning. When he is done with his meal, he leaves the napkin as it falls. Peter and John would have known this sign.

The risen Lord showed himself to Mary Magdalene first when she returned later to the tomb. (John 20:11–18) He walked with two men on the road to Emmaus (Luke 24:13–35). They received the knowledge of His presence by surprise and reverential awe. Then, He appeared to the disciples that evening (John 20:19–22) and gave them a fresh impartation of the Holy Spirit. He saw the disciples at the seaside (John 21:1–14), and again, in the upper room (Luke 24:36–49) and (Mark 16:14–18). He converted his brothers when they saw Him, among 500 others (I Corinthians 15:6–7), with the truth of His risen presence.

Three days in the grave (Luke 24:46) and 37 days walking among them before He ascended to heaven. Having witnessed the ascension, the disciples went away joyful, full of faith, and more determined than ever to preach the Kingdom's good news. He instructed them to "tarry in Jerusalem until you are endued with power from on high" (Luke 23:49) before they watched Him ascend home to the Father. (Mark 16:19, Luke 24: 51, John 6:62, Acts 19:12).

Ten days later, at Pentecost, the disciples got a full dose of the Holy Spirit. All of them went on to preach with a passion. All, but John the Beloved, died a martyr's death. That is how convinced they were that Christ was risen, ascended to heaven, and yet lives in our hearts.

We, too, are born of the Spirit when we put our trust, faith, and belief in our risen Savior, Jesus Christ. The very same spirit living in Jesus, now lives in us!

> Romans 8:11: "But if the Spirit of Him that raised up Jesus from the dead dwells in you, He that raised up Christ from the dead

shall also quicken your mortal body by His Spirit that dwells in you."

That is with all power and authority! Freely given—we didn't earn it by our works, only by believing. Christ earned it for us. He paid our sin debt and made us free! Hallelujah! Glory to His Name! We have His righteousness before the Father God. Calling on His name with His power living in us gives us victory over the temptation to sin and takes away our guilt and shame (we are loved and forgiven). All because we believe His blood sacrifice was accepted by Father God.

> Hebrews 10:12–18" "But this man, after He had offered one sacrifice for sins forever, sat down on the right hand of God 13 from henceforth expecting till His enemies be made His footstool. 14 For by one offering, He has perfected forever them that are sanctified. 15 Whereof the Holy Ghost also is a witness to us; for after that He had said before 16 This is the covenant that I will make with them after those days, saith the Lord, I will put my laws into their hearts, and in their minds will I write them 17 And their sins and iniquities will I remember no more. 18 Now where remission of these is, there is no more offering for sin."

Just imagine His reception in Heaven when He ascended to the Father. Hallelujah!

All the host of Heaven received Him with cheers of gladness! The radiance of His Glory shining brighter than the sun, we will see someday if we don't turn back.

Don't turn back!

> II Peter 2:20–21: "For if, after they have escaped the pollutions of the world through the knowledge of the Lord and Savior Jesus Christ, they are again entangled therein and overcome, the latter end is worse with them than the beginning. 21 For it had been better for them not to have known the way of righteousness, than, after they have known it, to turn from the holy commandment delivered unto them."

> Hebrews 6:4–6: "For it is impossible for those who were once enlightened and have tasted of the heavenly gift, and were made partakers of the Holy Ghost, 5 And have tasted the good Word of God, and the powers of the world to come 6 If they shall fall away, to renew them again unto repentance, seeing they crucify to themselves the Son of God afresh and put Him to an open shame."

As the Creator of all things made (Genesis 1:1, John 1:3, and Romans 4:17), including time, gravity, and all physical laws of matter and nature—the Holy Trinity is not subject to those laws, They are present at all times. The Triune Godhead is omni-everything!

This is why Jesus' sacrifice satisfies all past, present, and future sins. He is present in our lives every moment now, as much as He was on the cross. And we, because His Spirit lives in us, were there with Him. We were buried with Him and rose again to new life the moment we accepted His person. Spirits are eternal beings.

Having His Holy Spirit living inside of us is our best witness to the truth of the Gospel. The Spirit gives us gifts of His choosing, like council and wisdom. He gave C. Austin Miles, the writer of the 1912 hymn "In The Garden," the creative wisdom to write these words,

> "And He walks with me, and He talks with me, And He tells me I am His own." While receiving the insight to write this hymn, he shook and reverently thought, "It is the daily companionship with the Lord that makes up the Christian life (St Augustine, Record).

CHAPTER SIX

SAUL BECOMES PAUL

This great mystery, the sacrifice of Jesus to take away the sins of the world, was revealed to Paul after his conversion. Let's begin at the beginning with Saul before his name was changed to Paul.

NOTE: Matt Vila noticed Abram was a Gentile name that God changed to Hebrew, as Abraham. Where Saul was a Hebrew name, God changed to a Gentile name, Paul. Abraham began a new covenant era with God, and Saul did, too, explaining the New Testament of grace.

Tutored for years in his youth to become a Pharisee, Saul learned the Law at the feet of the very best teacher of the day. Saul knew as much and as well as any of the Council of that day and thought himself zealous for Almighty God.

Saul became the main tormentor of those people of "The Way," as the followers of Jesus were called. Those early followers of the risen Savior were beaten by Saul to blasphemy (curse) the Name of Jesus or be hauled into prison, tortured, or killed.

Those escaping Saul's grasp did spread the Word of Jesus as they fled to the uttermost parts of the known world.

His conversion was on the road to Damascus to seek out more followers of The Way. Acts Chapter 9 gives a good account of how Saul was blinded by a bright light—at noon—when the sun was already at its peak. Then Saul heard a voice from the light identifying Himself, "I am Jesus . . . " (Acts 9:5).

Now Saul is trembling (9:6), remembering all he had done to His followers. Saul had to be saying to himself, "They were right! He's alive and speaking to me from heaven." He had to be wondering, then, what Jesus was going to do with him.

Our merciful Savior let him become blind for three days while Ananias was fetched to pray for his healing (Acts 9:10–19). So sweet it makes me cry when I hear Ananias say, "Brother, Saul." Later, we read in Galatians Chapter 1 what happened next.

Remember, Luke wrote the book of Acts and reported what he understood to come after Saul was healed. Luke wasn't present. With his next verse, Acts 9:20 Paul is preaching in Damascus. That preaching came after meeting with Christ for a personal lesson in grace, according to Saul, who became Paul, who wrote Galatians.

So, first hand, we read in Galatians that Paul did not discuss or learn from any man, only with Christ, in the desert of Arabia. Our teacher, Matthew, thinks the place in Arabia where he met with the Lord may very well be Mt. Sinai. That would be an appropriate place to meet with Jesus for three years to learn about the mystery.

> Galatians 1: 15–17: "But when it pleased (Father) God, who separated me from my mother's womb, and called me by His grace, 16 to reveal His Son to me, that I might preach Him among the heathen. Immediately, I conferred not with flesh and blood. 17 Neither went I up to Jerusalem to them which were apostles before me, but I went into Arabia, and returned again unto Damascus."

To teach there his newfound lesson of Christ's true purpose of being born of a virgin, living a sinless life, giving Himself as a sacrifice to forgive all sin, resurrecting Himself, and ascending to His Father.

The entire book of Ephesians, also written by Paul to the people of Ephesus, is endearing, enlightening and full of nuggets worth memorizing. Ephesians 3:1–12 is where we find another account of what happened directly after Paul was healed of blindness (Sunday school notes in parenthesis).

Ephesians 3:1–12: "For this cause (to teach and edify the believers in Christ) I, Paul, the prisoner of Jesus Christ (Paul wrote this letter from a prison in Rome) for you Gentiles. 2 If you have heard of the dispensation (teaching for this time period) of the grace of God (the free gift of salvation by faith in Jesus as the Messiah/the Christ. His free-will gift to us—we didn't earn it—it's a gift given to those who believe) which is given (from) me to you-ward. 3 How that by revelation He made known unto me the Mystery (the secret purpose of the cross). As I wrote afore in few words (see Galatians above) 4 Whereby, when you read, you may understand my knowledge in the mystery of Christ. 5 Which in other ages was not made known (Grace was never prophesied in the Old Testament. Remember, it was a secret hidden from Satan from the beginning of our time when Adam and Eve sinned. The blood shed of the—was probably a lamb—covered them, atoned for them, but could not actually pay a sin debt. The Lamb—or animal sacrificed—was a precursor, a hint of Christ to come). 6 That the Gentiles should be fellow heirs, (with the Jews) and of the same body, and partakers of His promise in

Christ by the gospel, 7 Whereof I was made a minister according to the gift of the grace of God (Pauls' life was spared on the road to Damascus) given unto me by the effectual working of His power (blinded then healed). 8 Unto me, who am less than the least of all saints, (humbled from his treacherous past) is this grace given, that I should preach among the Gentiles the unsearchable riches of Christ (Glory!) 9 And to make all men see what is the fellowship (neither Jew, nor Greek, nor . . . we are all children of God – joint heirs) of the mystery which from the beginning of the world hath been hid (was a secret) in God, who created all things by Jesus Christ (See John 1:3). 10 to the intent that now, unto the principalities and powers in heavenly places (the angels didn't know either) might be known by the church the manifold wisdom of God (Hallelujah!) 11 According to the eternal purpose which He (Father God) purposed in Christ Jesus our Lord 12 In Whom (Father God) we have boldness and access with confidence by the faith of Him (Jesus)."

Jesus tore the veil at His point of death so we may boldly come before the mercy seat (throne) of God, anytime. What most Christians fail to realize today, though, is that the disciples of Jesus were still practicing Jews! Even when they wrote most of their books for the New Testament, they taught the Kingdom as Jesus did.

One must divide what was spoken before the cross (the law) from the grace that came after the cross. The necessity of 'rightly dividing," first mentioned by Paul in a letter to Timothy, comes into play when we hear what Christ had to say to the Jews, as well as the lessons from the prophets in the Old Testament and to understand, that was about the works of the law.

> II Timothy 2:15: "Study to show thyself approved unto God, a workman that needs not to be ashamed, rightly dividing the Word of truth."

Our teacher, Matt, taught us how to rightly divide the Word of Truth. This is an important concept because it makes sense of what was written, according to these three things. The three questions one must ask when considering what we read in the Holy Bible are:

1) Who said it?

2) To whom was it spoken?

3) When was it spoken—before or after the (speaker learned about) the cross?

Those answers decide if what is written is about the law before the cross, or of the grace after the cross. That is an important distinction because, as Matt says, "All of the Bible was written for us, but not all of it was written to us."

Paul's journeys are well-documented, beginning after Arabia starting in Damascus. Historically, he is considered the apostle to the Gentiles. At first, he taught in the synagogues to the Jews and the few Gentiles attending. The Gentiles were more receptive than the Jews to receive the gospel of grace.

When Paul said the new covenant of grace allowed Gentiles to become sons of God, fellow heirs, with all the good promises of God, and they did not have to follow the Law or be circumcised—well, this caused an uproar among the Orthodox Jews, the Old Testament kind, who believed all 613 laws must be met.

Paul was driven from many of the towns he visited by angry Orthodox Jews. With so much persecution, Paul spoke then, mainly to Gentiles {Lambert: Think how God used Saul as a perfect example of Grace. Saul was the worst of the Jews toward Christians. Then, he was forgiven and used by God to lead them into grace and glory}.

Meanwhile, the plan of God was explained by Peter to a house full of Gentiles, as he was summoned to preach Christ at the home of Cornelius in Acts Chapter 10:1–48. Peter had a vision to go, with the Spirit saying, they are at the door to ask you now (Acts 10:19–20).

Peter began by explaining to Cornelius that, as a Jew, it was unlawful for him to be in the home of . . . "one of another nation . . . ." (verse 28). He was still operating under Old Testament Law.

While Peter was speaking of Christ as the Messiah, the Holy Spirit fell on all those gathered at the home of Cornelius and they began to speak in tongues. Peter and the few Jews with him were astonished that these Gentiles had been given the gift of the Spirit, which was apparent. So, they baptized them, too.

It wasn't until Paul, who received the knowledge of the purpose of the cross from Christ Himself, who then passed that knowledge onto the disciples, so they heard the truth. It still took some time to settle it firmly in their minds, to undo what was ingrained from childhood. They eventually left the works of the Law behind and embraced that we are saved by grace alone. We can't earn it with following rules or by doing service.

Paul went to Jerusalem to share the teaching he received from Christ three years after receiving the wisdom. He told Peter first and later, some to James (the half-brother raised with Jesus), that new believers are saved by grace and not from following the law—a totally new concept to the converted Jew.

> Galatians 1:18–19: "Then after three years, I went up to Jerusalem to see Peter, and abode with him fifteen days. 19 But other of the apostles saw I none, save James, the Lord's brother."

Paul does not record what words he spoke to Peter and James. Most likely, he was describing his experience with Christ in the desert of Arabia. Paul would be telling them about the reason for the cross. It was a secret, not prophesied at all in the Old Testament. The cross was meant to erase all man's sins—past, present, and future. Surely, he spoke to them about having faith in who Jesus is. Just like he had been preaching to the Jews and Gentiles for the last three years, it is in believing what Jesus did for us, is what saves us, not doing the law of works.

Remember, the other disciples and Peter were still practicing Jews. They were probably still offering sacrifices at the temple, not realizing Christ was not just an innocent man crucified. He was THE sacrifice; the Holy, without sin, pure Lamb, made as a sacrifice for all sin, past, present, and future. No more sacrifices needed to be made, ever! Just look to Jesus. This was new news to them. Peter may have argued Christ had said nothing about it. (Yet, He did).

Jesus spared Paul's life, the one who tortured His followers. Paul was forgiven! Christ taught him personally, probably for three years or more in the desert. John the Baptist spent his youth in the desert, learning (Luke 1:80). Paul was a zealous preacher and would not have given up on Peter's understanding. This could be why Paul's visit took fifteen days.

Do you recall how the veil was torn in the temple at the moment of Christ's death? We know the significance, but Paul probably had to tell Peter that it represented free access to the Father. No longer needed was the High Priest, once a year, to go into the Holy of Holies with the blood of a bull to atone for our sins.

Matt picks up his Bible, pinching those few pages between Acts and Revelation. "There are two religions in this book, Judaism and Christianity, and we are just a small part of the entire Bible." Good point.

The New Testament begins with the death of Jesus. In Luke's rendition of the "Last Supper," Jesus declares,

> Luke 22:20: "This is the new testament in my blood, which is shed for you."

Any valid will and and testament begins with the death of the Testator. It can be altered up until that point. Our New Promise or Covenant is attached to this Testament. Part of our inheritance is the presence of His Holy Spirit to lead, guide, and teach us. His Holy Spirit lives inside believers! It was foretold in Jeremiah.

> Jeremiah 31:31–34: "Behold, the days come, saith the Lord, That I will make a new covenant with the house of Israel and with the house of Judah: 32 Not according to the covenant that I made with their fathers in the day I took them by the hand to bring them out of the land of Egypt; Which

my covenant they broke, although I was a husband unto them, saith the Lord. 33 But this shall be the covenant I will make with the house of Israel; After those days, saith the Lord, I will put my law in their inward parts, and write it in their hearts, and will be their God and they shall be my people. 34 And they shall teach no more every man his neighbor and every man his brother saying, Know the Lord; For they shall all know me, from the least of them unto the greatest of them, saith the Lord. For I will forgive their iniquity and I will remember their sin no more."

The Old Covenant Laws proved you could not be perfect, as mentioned in Hebrews 8:7–13. The Law was perfect, but Israel could not keep it. Nor could we have.

Hebrews 8:13: "In that (verses 7–12, a recant of Jeremiah above), He says, a new covenant, He has made the first old. Now that which decays and waxes old is ready to vanish away."

After the cross, there is no need for the Law. First, we received His forgiveness; then, like the woman who washed the feet of Jesus with her tears, out of love, we obey. Jesus said in John 14:15, "If you love me, keep my commandments."

We have His Holy Spirit living in us, breathing new life into us to lead and correct us. Chapter 9 of Hebrews further explains the furnishings of the Tabernacle and how Christ fulfilled these things.

> Hebrews 9:13–14: "For if the blood of bulls and of goats, and the ashes of a heifer sprinkling the unclean, sanctifies to the purifying of the flesh 14 How much more shall the blood of Christ, who through the eternal Spirit offered himself without spot to God, purge your conscience from dead works to serve the living God?"

AMEN

With the Old Covenant, blessings came by obedience. (Deuteronomy 6:24–25). If you do not obey, you may expect a curse (Deuteronomy 11:26).

When God forgives you of your sins, that is not a demonstration of His love and mercy but of justice. Because that was all paid for at the cross. He must forgive. The demonstration of His love and mercy was giving us His Son to make that exchange for our benefit.

> John 3:16: "For God so loved the world that He gave His only begotten Son, that whosoever believes in Him shall not perish but have everlasting life."

> I John 4:10: "Herein is love, not that we loved God but that He loved us and sent His Son to be the propitiation (substitute) for our sins."

After fourteen years of teaching the Gentiles grace by faith, not works, Paul returned to Jerusalem to attend the Jerusalem Council. This is the event convened to settle the guidelines a new believers would be told concerning what they needed to do to live like they have been saved. Many speakers had something to say. Circumcision was a crucial point of debate brought into question by converted Jews who still had not perfected the idea of being saved by grace (the free gift from Christ) by faith in His sacrifice—and not by their works of following laws.

> Galatians 2:16: "Knowing that a man is not justified by the works of the law, but by faith of Jesus Christ . . . for by the works of the law shall no flesh be justified."

Once a headstrong Pharisee, Paul knew the Torah and all the prophets. There was no debating him. Between his first journey to Jerusalem to speak with Peter and this trip, Paul had been around—literally covering much terra firma. Teaching, preaching, and making converts from pagan religions, idol worshipers, and some Jews, Paul established churches, gained followers, and got in a whole lot of trouble doing it.

Orthodox Jews and some newly converted would follow after Paul left an area to undo the Word of grace and insist the Gentiles be circumcised and follow the laws of Moses.

Grace cannot be mixed with works. It is by faith alone in Christ alone. He had to stress this at the Jerusalem Council. Paul learned his new doctrine from Christ Himself, that:

> Ephesians 2:8–10: "For by grace are you saved, through faith and that not of yourselves, it is the gift of God. 9 Not of works, lest any man should boast. 10 For we are His workmanship, created in Christ Jesus unto good works, (serving others) which God had before ordained that we should walk in them (flowing from a grateful heart)."

At the conclusion of the Jerusalem Council, letters went out by the hands of men with Barnabas and Paul, saying:

> Acts 15:23–29: "And they wrote letters by them after this manner; The apostles and elders and brethren send greeting unto the

brethren which are of the Gentiles in Antioch and Syria and Cilicia. 24 Forasmuch as we have heard, that certain (Jewish converts) which went out from us have troubled you with words, subverting your souls, saying, "you must be circumcised and keep the law," to whom we gave no such commandment. 25 It seemed good unto us, being assembled with one accord . . . 28 For it seemed good to the Holy Ghost, and to us, to lay upon you no greater burden than these necessary things: 29 That you abstain from meats offered to idols, and from blood (a pagan ritual of drinking—not meaning a rare steak) and from things strangled, and from fornication: from which, if you keep yourselves, you shall do well. Fare ye well."

Little by little, grace, not works, became a way of life for the followers of Jesus. We know habits engrained from a young age are hard to break. Some doctrine became muddled at first, for the Jews turned Christian.

And for us, these days? We, too, may have learned other doctrines and rules. There are currently 41,000 different denominations out there. Some perversions of the truth of the Holy Bible are interpreted differently. It is important to get to the truth God intended. Ask the Spirit to guide you. Scripture confirms scripture, so look for it.

For instance, the book of James was written urging works as a testament of faith. James 2:14 says, "What does it profit, my brethren though a man say he has faith and has not works? Can faith save him?"

Yes, James! Only faith can save us. Works promote self-righteousness. That's prideful. Works presume God owes that person salvation for what they did for Him. Paul answers in Romans Chapter 11 about the Orthodox Jews who love God.

> Romans 11:6: "And if (we are saved) by grace, then it is no more of works . . . .

Saying further in the chapter that the Jews who don't accept this grace yet are made blind to it as part of the plan of God for the salvation of the Gentiles."

> Romans 11:25: " . . . that blindness partly happened to Israel until the fullness of the Gentiles came in."

James also mentions Abraham for the works he (almost) did, offering Isaac as a sacrifice (James 2:21–24). It was Abraham's faith, believing in the promise God gave him to become a nation through Isaac, that urged his obedience to God's command. Abraham trusted God knew what He was asking, not doubting a moment but believing all along in the promise God made him. So, as

James speaks of Abraham's intense faith, he also lauds his works. We can, too.

James probably heard about grace on Paul's first trip to Jerusalem, when Paul spent 15 days with Peter. Evidently, the free gift (grace) of believing (faith) in what Jesus accomplished on the cross didn't sink in completely or change his old ways until several years later.

Maybe, when Paul returned concerning the "Jerusalem Council." Yes, faith in the finished work on the cross is all that can save you.

In I Peter, Peter stresses good behavior, as well as love and adoration for the sacrifice of Jesus. Ending II Peter, he says, listen to Paul, too.

> II Peter 3:13–18: "Nevertheless, we, according to His promise, look for new heavens and a new earth, wherein dwells righteousness. 14 Wherefore, beloved, seeing that you look for such things, be diligent that you may be found of Him in peace, without spot and blameless. 15 and account that the longsuffering of our Lord is salvation; even as our beloved brother Paul also, according to the wisdom given unto him has written unto you. 16 As also in all his epistles, speaking in them of these things . . . (some hard to understand by the unlearned, as other scriptures. Don't be led away. Keep

> your steadfastness). 18 Grow in grace, and in the knowledge of our Lord and Savior Jesus Christ. To Him be glory both now and forever. Amen."

An excellent example of rightly dividing the Word of truth is in Matthew, with words written in red, spoken by our Lord.

> Matthew 6:14: "For if you forgive men their trespasses, your heavenly Father will also forgive you. 15 But if you forgive not men their trespasses, neither will your Father forgive your trespasses."

Jesus was teaching with Old Testament law to the Jewish people surrounding Him before the cross. He may have been referring to "an eye for an eye" in Deuteronomy. Now we know that forgiving someone who hurt you, who sinned against God by hurting you, gives you peace. There will still be a Judgment Day when He will settle the score. Not forgiving those who hurt you leaves you with bitter resentment, an unhealthy way to live out your end.

Jesus also taught us to see the love of the Father and trust Him.

> Matthew 5:44–45: " . . . I say unto you. Love your enemies, bless them that curse you,

do good to them that hate you, and pray for them which despitefully use you, and persecute you; 45 That you may be the children of your Father which is in heaven, for He makes His sun rise on the evil and on the good and sends rain on the just and on the unjust."

The cross changed everything. Your sins are forgiven.

Thank You, Jesus, for your obedience, and thank you, Father God, for the plan. From the point of the cross onward, any disobedience from believers is also erased, covered by the blood Jesus shed for them. Consequences naturally follow actions. That's a natural law of reaping what we sow. This we will experience.

Paul says in Colossians 3:13:

"Forbearing one another, and forgiving one another, if any man have a quarrel against any, even as Christ forgave you, so also do ye."

Within the teachings of Paul, we see how our sins are forgiven; that does not, however, give us a license to sin. He was adamant about that in the book of Romans, especially chapter 7:15–25, where we see how Paul has a will to do well because he was born again with a new Spirit nature, but in his soul, the flesh nature still wishes to give in to sin.

In verses 21–23, three laws work. The Old Testament Law of God is mentioned twice, before the Law of the Holy Spirit, which gives us wisdom and power to be victorious. Then, the Law of the mind, which is the fleshy, innate sin nature, is used twice.

> Romans 7: 21–23 (Paul speaking): "I find then a law, that, when I would do good (when I want to do good), evil is present with me (still) 22 For I delight in the law of God after the inward man: 23 But I see another law (the Spirit) in my members warring against the law of my mind and bringing me into captivity to the law of sin which is in my members."

To the degree you give yourself to the flesh (wrath, wanton sex, doubt, fear, etc.), you open the door and give control to the devil's minions to the point that you can't control yourself; they control you. Your weakness is their door.

They observe you to find that weakness. Traumatic experiences weaken your will, and so does the bitterness of unforgiveness. They use your experiences to corrupt your knowledge with small, twisted lies whispered to deceive you. You don't know you are being deceived when you believe the lie. You think it is the truth. That stirs your emotions to anger, doubt, and fear.

The mind is our soul, which is considered to be our personality, emotions, intellect, and will. Matthew Vila says the soul is our report card, unique to every individual. It contains a record of our decisions based on our knowledge and experiences at the time. This record is always developing as we mature.

Jesus says of the Spirit in the book of John:

> John 6:63 "It is the Spirit that quickens (ripens your spiritual fruit) the flesh profits nothing. The Words I speak unto you, they are Spirit, and they are life."

Paul gives us keys to the victory spelled out for us so that the Spirit will win every time!

> Romans 8:1, 10: "There is therefore now no condemnation to them which are in Christ Jesus, who walk not after the flesh, but after the Spirit. 10 And if Christ be in you, the body is dead because of sin, but the Spirit is life because of righteousness."

> Romans 12:1–2: "I beseech you therefore, brethren, by the mercies of God, that you present your bodies a living sacrifice, holy, acceptable unto God, which is your reasonable service. 2 And be not conformed

> to this world but be ye transformed by the renewing of your mind, that you may prove what is that good and acceptable and perfect will of God."
>
> Luke 11:13: "How much more shall your heavenly Father give the Holy Spirit to them that ask him?"

There it is. How to live holy with His Holy Spirit in us, giving us the power not to sin. We walk in a newness of life, renewing our minds by reading and thinking about the Word of God. The Spirit is always rejoicing in the glory of God. Let your soul (mind) and body do the same. Jump for joy! Feel free to ask God for more.

After the cross, anyone calling on the Name of the Lord Jesus with faith in his heart will be "born again" with the Holy Spirit living inside him to spend eternity in heaven! {Phil: Don't put it off, do it today, like there is no tomorrow. There might not be.}

It requires faith to believe in the righteousness we are given the moment we believe. Read all about it in His Word, the Bible, front to back. We have, living inside of us, the power and authority of Christ Jesus, and we are the picture of His Righteousness in the eyes of Father God.

{Keith: Our value of being obedient increases as our foundation of believing in our righteousness is affirmed. Quoting . . . }

> II Corinthians 5:21: "For He (the Father) has made Him (Jesus) to be sin for us, who knew no sin, that we might be made the righteousness of God in Him."

With our hearts full of gratitude for His expensive gift, all His blood shed from scourging and hanging—our humble thanks is to want to be just like Him, in Word and deed. Willingly, we sacrifice our wants for His service. With His spirit in us, we become His hands and feet. That's walking in His Spirit.

Or, like a seed sown in the ground, Jesus told the disciples this parable to explain His death and show the rewards of our servant's heart when we share His Gospel and do for others.

> John 12:24–26: "Verily, verily, I say into you, Except a corn of wheat fall into the ground and die, it abides alone; but if it die, it brings forth much fruit. He that loves his (earthly) life shall lose it (eternal life in heaven) and he that hates his life in this world (will exchange it for His will) shall keep it unto life eternal. If any man serve Me, let him follow

Me and where I am, (heaven) there shall also My servant be. If any man serve Me, him will my Father honor."

This is where works come in for the believer. They come as service out of a loving heart full of gratitude. We don't work at the food bank or give to the poor to earn our salvation. We already have that assurance. We do it with the spirit of thankfulness for the sacrifice Jesus made on our behalf. We do for others willingly and joyfully. Our works are a fruit of love, a result of loving God and others.

We tithe not because it is a commandment. We realize everything belongs to Father God. He gives us that job to earn our wages because He is a good Father, and this is His provision for us. We tithe in faith, knowing He will continue to ensure we have enough {Rosemary: My father told me not to look at the change in the offering plate or the fancy dress of the giver, but it was the heart that mattered}.

Just because thoughts come into your head is not a sin. It is only after we agree with the thought conception begins. This is why Paul says we need to kill the "old man," the person we were, with those bad habits we had before knowing Christ.

James 1:14: "But every man is tempted when he is drawn away of his own lust and

> enticed. 15 Then when lust has conceived, it brings forth sin. And sin, when it is finished, brings forth death."

You will be miserable if you are a believer and choose to live in sin. Think of sin as an allergy, like peanuts. You will stay far away from peanuts once you experience the reactions to eating them. The consequence of sin is death to your Spirit. Like Adam and Eve lost their Shakina glory (Heavenly glow) to discover they were naked.

This house you live in is not you. Your body only houses the flesh nature. Reckon it dead. Feed your Spirit man, by reading the Word and mulling it throughout your day (No time to worry). Walk in the Spirit. Your body is considered the temple, where Jesus lives in your heart. Put away the works of the flesh mentioned in Galatians 5:19–21 and nurture the fruits of the Spirit (Galatians 5:22–23).

> Galatians 5:16: "Walk in the Spirit and you shall not fulfill the lust of the flesh."

Jesus told the Samaritan woman at the well (This was an actual occurrence, not a parable) in John 4:23–24:

> "But the hour cometh and now is, when the true worshippers shall worship the Father in spirit and in truth; for the Father seeks such to worship Him. 24 God is a Spirit, and they

> that worship Him must worship Him in spirit and truth."

After the ascension of Jesus, the gift of the Holy Spirit came to believers to teach us, counsel us, and empower us to do God's will (Acts 1:4–5, 8–14; 2:1–10). Paul spoke mightily in I Corinthians 2: 1–16.

> I Corinthians 2:11–12: "For what man knows the things of a man, save the spirit of man, which is in him? Even so, the things of God knows no man, but the Spirit of God (knows). 12 Now, we have received, not the spirit of the world, but the spirit which is of God; that we might know the things that are freely given to us of God."

With the endowment of His Holy Spirit living in believers, the rise of Christianity became great. It got even better after Saul's conversion to Paul—so much so that the Pharisees were out to get him.

With the same vengeance they had for Jesus of Nazareth, the Pharisees wanted to do away with Paul. They plotted to kill him, but Paul always managed to escape. Lastly, by appealing to Caesar, as Paul was born in Rome, a new journey began for him (See Acts 23:11 to the end of Acts). Paul endured many tribulations along the way to Rome, yet his joy was great!

No longer able to travel, Paul wrote most of his epistles (letters) from confinement in Rome, enthusiastically addressing many of the churches he had started and the people he taught personally. Timothy was one of those people. Paul affectionately called him his son. He told Timothy to rightly divide the Word of Truth and reminded him to stay strong in his faith.

When Paul was martyred, about 65 AD, his death coincided with the transition period of 40 years (a generation) to get the Old Testament Law out of converted Jews, who became believers after the death of Christ about 33 AD and to get grace as the center of their lives (although the process still continues today).

In 70 AD, the Romans destroyed the second temple in Jerusalem by fire. (The first temple was built by Solomon. The second was built with the return of people from 70 years in captivity. See the books of Ezra and Nehemiah). This destruction was a major factor in the transition period. Sacrifices ceased, with no temple.

Jesus foretold this destruction:

> Luke 21:6 "As for these things which you behold (the temple), the days will come, in the which there shall not be left one stone upon another, that shall not be thrown down."

The Orthodox Jews of today would like to build another one and will, no doubt, accomplish it. Prophecy in Daniel 9 says an "abomination" will be sacrificed to signal the last half of the tribulation.

The great prophecy revealed to Daniel, who was in Babylonian captivity at the time he wrote; what we read as chapter 9 confirms the prophet Jeremiah concerning 70 weeks (years) in captivity for the disobedient Israelites. Daniel begins at verse 4 to pray for the sins of their nation, all the way through verse 19. He reveals at (9:13) that no one prayed "that we might turn from our iniquities." So, that is why Daniel prayed so earnestly.

In verses 16–19, Daniel pleads with God to "shine upon Thy sanctuary" in Jerusalem "and restore what is desolate" (this is just before the second temple was rebuilt with Ezra). While he was praying, the angel Gabriel came to explain the meaning of the "sentence."

> Daniel 9:24 (Gabriel speaking): "Seventy weeks are determined upon they people and upon thy holy city, to finish the transgression and to make an end of sins ... 25 Know therefore and understand that from the going forth of the commandment to restore and to build Jerusalem (for what Daniel just prayed was soon to happen) unto the Messiah the Prince shall be seven weeks, and threescore and two weeks: (7 + 62) the street shall be built again and the wall, even in troublous times. (See Nehemiah). 26 And after

threescore and two weeks shall Messiah be cut off, but not for himself: (Christ died for us, finishing the 69th week)."

The 70th week is coming—only God knows when exactly. Week 70 begins the seven-year tribulation period.

CHAPTER SEVEN

THE SEVEN FEASTS REVEALED

Leviticus 23 tells us about each of the seven feasts. Every major event in Christ's life was on a feast day.

Spring has three feasts, Summer one, and Fall has three feasts. Think of the seven lamps on the menorah. Three lamps on the left, one in the center, and three on the right.

In each of these three sections, comes one feast day, declared as a harvest feast. So, three times a year, in Spring, Summer, and Fall, all males over the age of 20 must bring their harvest, the requirements for that feast, to the temple for the priest to offer to God on his behalf.

> Deuteronomy 16:16: "In a year shall all thy males appear before the Lord thy God in the place which he shall choose, (written before they came into the Promised Land) in the feast of unleavened bread, and in the feast of weeks, and in the feast of

tabernacles and they shall not appear before the Lord empty."

The first feast of the year begins with the memorial of the Passover on the 14th day of the first month when the Israelites were rescued from the bondage of Egypt (Leviticus 23: 1–5).

Jesus was our innocent Passover Lamb and thereby fulfilled the first Spring Feast. He went to the cross without complaint as a lamb to the slaughter.

The very next day is the feast of Unleavened bread to be held for seven days with the first day being a Sabbath, a Holy Convocation where no work was to be done (Leviticus 23:5–8). Leaven is a symbol of sin used in Biblical passages. All leaven was to be removed and swept out of dwellings. There was to be no leaven in your home these seven days.

Jesus was without sin (no leaven). Jesus also fulfilled this feast at the cross, as He died without personal sin.

The third of the Spring feasts is a harvest celebration, the feast of First Fruits. (Leviticus 23:9–14). Within a field of grain, some sprigs will ripen early. Gathering these few plants together into a bundle, or sheath, is the offering of first fruits. Each male over 20 years old was required to bring their sheath to the priest to wave before the Lord in the temple.

Jesus fulfilled the First Fruits offering as the first to rise Himself from the grave.

> I Corinthians 15:20 "But now is Christ risen from the dead and become the first fruits of them that slept (died)."

When He died, there was an earthquake, and certain graves of the prophets were opened. When the resurrected body of Jesus emerged from the grave, so did those of the prophets. They were seen in the temple by many. Scripture also says,

> Matthew 27:50–53: "Jesus, when He had cried again with a loud voice, yielded up the ghost. 51 And, behold, the veil of the temple was rent in two, from the top to the bottom, and the earth did quake, and the rocks rent; 52 And the graves were opened, and many bodies of the saints which slept arose 53 And came out of the graves after his resurrection, and went into the holy city and appeared unto many."

So, there was a "sheath" of the first fruits, all resurrected from the grave. This is a sign for us. We, too, can expect a resurrected body, also called a glorified body. A resurrected body is equal to the angels. So says Jesus.

> Luke 20:35–36: "But they which shall be accounted worthy to obtain that world and the resurrection from the dead, neither marry nor are given in marriage 36 Neither can they die anymore, for they are equal unto the angels and are the children of God, being the children of the resurrection."

The resurrected body cannot die. It houses our eternal spirit, lives forever and can go from heaven to earth. Like in Jacob's ladder, his vision of the night is found in Genesis 28:10–16.

> Genesis 28:12: "And he dreamed, and behold a ladder set up on the earth and the top of it reached to heaven and behold the angels of God ascending and descending on it."

Also of note, at the point of death on the cross, the veil covering the Holy of Holies was rent in two. Scholars signify this means there is no barrier between us and the Father. Our Matt supposes, with the body of Jesus still on the cross, the Spirit of Jesus tore the veil in the earthly temple and went into the Holy of Holies in Heaven, the throne room of Almighty God, to present His sacrificed blood on the mercy seat of the throne. Jesus is our High Priest now, after the order of Melchizedek. His blood had made the ultimate sacrifice, once for forever! (He can only physically die once).

> Leviticus 17:11: "For the life of the flesh is in the blood and I have given it to you upon the altar to make an atonement for your souls: for it is the blood that makes an atonement for the soul."

> Hebrews 9:22: "And almost all things are by the law purged with blood; and without shedding of blood is no remission."

Following the three feasts of the spring season is the only summer feast when most of the crops are harvested. Often called the Feast of Weeks, or Pentecost, celebrating the 50th day since Jesus was resurrected and waiting, as Jesus instructed them just before He ascended to the Father. Waiting for what they did not know until the coming of the Holy Ghost, as He is called in the New Testament, coming to the disciples and followers in the Upper Room. What a glorious day!

Centered around the main harvest of the year. Explained in Leviticus 19 is how to reap this crop.

> Leviticus 19:9–10: "And when you reap the harvest of your land, you shall not wholly

reap the corners of your field, neither shall you gather the gleanings of the harvest. 10 And you shall not glean your vineyard, neither gather every grape of your vineyard, you shall leave them for the poor and stranger. I am the Lord your God."

Then, Leviticus 23 explains the timing of this feast at Pentecost. After the spring harvest of the First fruits, those few ripe stems, the field is given 50 days to ripen to maturity fully.

Leviticus 23:15–16: "And you shall count unto you from the morrow after the sabbath, from the day that you brought the sheaf of the wave offering: seven sabbaths shall be complete. 16 Even unto the morrow after the seven sabbath shall you number fifty days and you shall offer a new meat offering unto the Lord."

The workers have already been picking their crops leaving the four corners and anything they drop along the way for the gleaning of the poor and the stranger. They bring their offering to the priest from their harvest to offer at Pentecost with leavened bread (verse 23:17) and choice livestock (verses 18–19).

This feast of Pentecost is the only feast on which leavened bread is offered with the grain to the priests in the temple. This is a significant difference from the other feasts and our first clue to the Rapture. We are the main harvest.

God accepted the bread made with leaven, representing sin because we are saved by grace. We are not sinless; only Christ is. There was no grace before the cross. It was only, "Obey, and I will bless you."

The cross made grace possible for believers in the sacrifice of our Lamb, Jesus. God accepts us as we are because His Son's work on the cross exchanged our sins for His righteousness. Father God looks at us and sees His Son's righteousness.

We know God always does monumental things on feast days. The fact that the summer harvesters were not allowed to gather from the four corners, or the grain dropped in the harvest will be explained with the fall harvest feast.

Let's review the mystery of the two resurrections yet to come, as Paul reveals in I Corinthians 15. This is right after he argues his declaration of resurrection to those who did not believe in resurrection at all. He says, if there is no resurrection from the dead, then Christ died in vain, and your faith is worthless (verses 12–19).

> I Corinthians 15:20–26: "But now is Christ risen from the dead and (has) become the

firstfruits of them that slept (died). 21 For since by man (Adam) came death, by man (Christ) came also the resurrection of the dead. 22 For as in Adam all die, even so in Christ shall all be made alive. 23 But every man in his own order. (original Hebrew word meaning appointed time). Christ the firstfruits; (then) afterward, they that are Christ's at His coming (the Rapture). 24 Then, (after that event) comes the end, (the Tribulation), when he shall have delivered up the kingdom to God, even the Father; (then is) when He shall have put down all (Satan's earthly) rule and all authority and power. 25 For He must reign, till He has put all enemies under His feet. 26 The last enemy shall be destroyed is death. (Between verses 25 and 26, Satan is chained underground for 1000 years. See also Revelation 20:1–3)."

What we read then is about two resurrections to come. One is the Rapture, where Christ comes for His body of believing Christians. The second resurrection is when Christ returns for those who remained through the Tribulation.

We are living in the age of Grace. It began at Jesus's cross and has lasted over 2,000 years. How much longer before the Rapture and the seven-year tribulation begin? Only God knows.

We don't know when. We know next up on the God Calendar is the Rapture, when Jesus will come to get His bride. This is the body of Christ, the tried-and-true believers who walk the straight and narrow, whose faith in the Trinity is their foundation. Our salvation comes from believing what Jesus did on the cross.

Paul calls the first group of Raptured people the "Bride of Christ" because of the similarities of the Jewish wedding ritual. Once betrothed, the bridegroom goes to his father's house to prepare a place for his bride. She has no clue when he will return for her. When he comes for her, it is with a party of his "friends" of the bridegroom, and they are noisy. Then, he takes her to the place prepared at his father's house. Sound familiar? John 14:1–3.

> John 14:3: "And if I go and prepare a place for you, I will come again and receive you unto myself; that where I am, there you may be also."

He is speaking to those who believe we are saved by the work of Christ, not on our good works or service or of keeping the law. Only on the blood sacrifice of Christ, to forgive away our sins.

We don't deserve eternal life in heaven on our merits. We can't earn it. It is a free gift to accept at the Hand of Christ. He gave Himself for us. We cannot make ourselves holy. He paid for our sin as our substitute. And exchanged our "filthy rags" for His righteous standing with Father God. When God sees us, He sees the righteousness of an obedient Son. We are wholly forgiven! And has given us His Holy Spirit the moment we choose to believe.

To believe is to come to the knowledge and carry it wherever you go. You may tell yourself and any who will listen, "I have the righteousness of Christ." It comes with power.

His Spirit will live in us to guide us and to whisper wisdom. It may seem like an idea just popped into your head. Think about it. Where did you come up with knowledge you didn't know? You can enhance His presence by dwelling in His Word.

{debi—I believe from personal experience that a temporary glimmer of the Holy Spirit, or maybe angels, can come to the aid of unbelievers, who are covered by the prayers of believers, as a limited gift of knowledge or protection. God honors the prayers of His saints. I also believe this only happens to those who God knows will become believers in time.}

From the words of Paul, we see the timing of the Rapture occurs after Christ's resurrection and before the seven-year tribulation period.

> Romans 5:9: "Much more then (Father's love for us), being now justified by His blood, we shall be saved from wrath through Him."

> I Thessalonians 1:10: "And (we are) to wait for His Son from heaven whom He raised from the dead, even Jesus, which delivered us from the wrath to come. (Believing in Him is our ticket out of here before the Tribulation)."

The Rapture will happen before the tribulation because Father God is a good and gracious God. He has never let His beloved suffer His wrath for the ungodly. Scripture says so plainly.

Enoch ("E-nock") represents the raptured. He was born on Pentecost and was translated on the day of Pentecost.

> Genesis 5:23–24: "And all the days of Enoch were three hundred sixty and five years 24 And Enoch walked with God, and he was not, for God took him."

As an exceptional example, Noah demonstrates God's mercy of the just by saving seven other souls with him out of the entire Earth's population.

There's Lot. Abraham pleaded with the angels sent to destroy Sodom and Gomorrah, where his nephew, Lot, lived.

> Genesis 18:23" "And Abraham drew near, and said, Will you also destroy the righteous with the wicked?" Abraham bartered with the angels down to ten righteous; they would

> not destroy the city. But there were not even ten (Genesis 19:15–17). The angels escorted Lot, his wife, and two unwed daughters out of the city before raining fire and brimstone.

The life of Jonah was spared—his mission was not yet accomplished. God even provided his transportation to Nineveh.

And Elijah was spared from famine. We can derive much faith from his story, from the God of provision (I Kings 17).

> I Kings 17: 4, 6: "And it shall be, you shall drink of the brook, and I have commanded the ravens to feed you there. 6 And the ravens brought him bread and flesh in the morning and bread and flesh in the evening, and he drank of the brook."

When it was his time to leave Earth, Elijah didn't die. He was carried off to heaven in a fiery chariot (II Kings 2:11) that swooped down from heaven in a whirlwind and picked him up. Maybe he jumped in. Anyway, way to go!

Before those dreadful days of the Tribulation, the church, the body of believers of Christ, His Bride, will be taken up in our glorified bodies and saved from this wrath.

> I Thessalonians 4:14–17: "For if we believe that Jesus died and rose again, even so them

also which sleep in Jesus (believers passed away and buried) will God bring with Him. 15 For this we say unto you by the Word of the Lord, that we which are alive and remain unto the coming of the Lord shall not prevent them which are asleep. (who have died before us). 16 For the Lord Himself shall descend from heaven with a shout, with the voice of the archangel and with the trump of God, and the dead in Christ shall rise first; 17 Then we, which are alive and remain shall be caught up together with them in the clouds, to meet the Lord in the air and so shall we ever be with the Lord."

I Corinthians 15:52: "In a moment, in the twinkling of an eye, at the last trump. For the trumpet shall sound and the dead shall be raised incorruptible, and we shall be changed."

Not all Christians will be raptured. Only those who believe they are saved by grace alone in Christ alone—for His finished work on the cross. Many Christians today believe they are saved by grace and still need to . . . tithe, be baptized, take communion . . . . Those things are good Gospel principles but don't save you. If you put any faith in them, you are taking it away from Christ alone and counting on your works. Many good people go to church every Sunday. They put their tithes in the basket but will be left behind. Are you counting on your good deeds to save you? You can't mix works and grace.

Orthodox Jews won't be raptured. They didn't believe in Jesus at the time of His coming, and most still don't.

Some Jews have come to believe Jesus is the Messiah. How many of those Messianic Jews still follow some of the laws of the Old Testament? They count them as necessary for their righteousness, unaware you can't mix law and grace.

There are currently over 41,000 different religions in the world, based on one Bible. There is only one truth, with 41,000 perversions of it. Somehow, the Word is distorted or given a different meaning than what was intended.

What about atheists, hypocrites, those led astray, and kind-of-believers? They will endure the tribulation period. Only God knows our hearts. He is the judge. It seems these days that He is already separating the sheep from the goats.

The special thing about the Rapture is it will take out the saints Jesus is saving from the wrath to come. Then, the wrath will come.

As for the fall's feasts, all three are in the seventh month of the Jewish calendar. First up is the Feast of Trumpets on the first day of the month. Trumpets are blown to herald the beginning of the fall's feast and to signal the completion of the fall's crop harvest. This means all harvesting is officially over so the poor and the stranger may begin to glean those fields.

Ten days later is the Day of Atonement, when the high priest will offer a sacrifice for the nation. These ten days between the Trumpets blasting and the day of the atoning sacrifice is an opportunity for all the nation, especially heads of families, to reflect on their past behavior. They settle debts, forgive others, and ask for forgiveness. They come to Jerusalem, fasting and praying.

On the ninth day, many will be in sackcloth with ashes on their heads. They want to be forgiven when the high priest offers the sacrifice on the altar.

On the 15th day is the Feast of Tabernacles, or Booths, to memorialize the time of the freed Hebrew slaves wandering in the wilderness in tents. Always prepared to pick up and move with the pillar of cloud by day (that gave them shade) or the pillar by night (to warm them on desert nights). When the pillar of God moved away from the "tent of meeting," His temporary tabernacle, the Israelites were to pack up quickly and move along with it.

CHAPTER EIGHT

TRIBULATION TO NEW HEAVEN

With the Body of Christ gone, who is going to stop the antichrist? No one. Most will embrace him and his culture.

> II Thessalonians 2:3: "Let no man deceive you by any means for that day shall not come, except there comes a falling away first (original Hebrew means—a departure—that's our rapture) and that man of sin be revealed, the son of perdition."

This period begins with the Antichrist making a peace treaty. That won't happen until the "restrainer" is removed. That is us, the spirit-filled church. We are the ones keeping back the evil plan of the Antichrist. With us gone, there will be no one to oppose him.

If you are opposed to that culture, good. Yet, you would be wise not to mention it. If you are asked, that's another story. You can't deny your love for Christ and expect to be blessed with eternal life in heaven. If the opposition lets you keep your head on your shoulders, good. If they slay you with your faith intact, you will be saved for heaven's eternity.

In light of the Rapture, if that should happen with the Summer Harvest of Pentecost, if we go up when the Holy Spirit first came down, *we are* the harvest of the main "crop." We left the gleaning and the four corners of the main crops for those who missed the Rapture to live through the time of the seven years of Tribulation. Christ will return for those precious souls, at His second coming.

Scripture says that if one becomes a believer during the tribulation period, and a few will, they have to hang onto their faith until the end. They will need to bless Israel and cannot take the mark of the beast.

These newest believers may be martyred for their faith, like many of the saints before them. Can you view martyrdom as a blessing? Eternity awaits everyone. The question is, where will you spend it?

With Christianity gone, the Old Testament laws will be in place again. The Jews will rebuild their temple. All sins will again require a sin offering. As a new believer in God, you must obey the law and bless Israel to be blessed. Israel will be the superpower in that time.

Psalm 83 says they will conquer all their bordering countries and, in effect, expand Israel's borders to the old Roman Empire. That's when Ezekiel chapters 38 and 39 will take effect when God intervenes and conquers the countries that think they will come to take the spoil of Israel.

The feast of Atonement would normally follow ten days after the feast of Trumpets in the seventh month, except at the mid-point of the seven-year tribulation period, when Daniel foretells us of the offering of sacrifice by the antichrist as an "abomination of desecration" will happen on the altar of the third temple (yet to be built). This is when the Antichrist will declare himself as God, making himself judge overall.

Whatever sacrifice desecrates the temple will begin the exodus of Jews from the area to flee to the wilderness, as spoken in Revelation 12, for the remaining three-and-a-half years, coinciding with the Feast of Tabernacles. These refugees will be living in temporary dwellings during this time. God intends to save the Orthodox Jews. They still are His chosen people.

> Revelation 12:6: "And the woman fled into the wilderness, where she had a place prepared of God, that they should feed her there a thousand two hundred and three score days. (3.48 years—the last half of the Tribulation)."

The Bible tells us in the end times will be catastrophic atmospheric events. The sun will be darkened, and the moon will not give its light, the majority of fish will die, and the seas will dry. One-third of the grass and trees will be burned up (Sounds like nuclear war, doesn't it?)

The trumpets sounding on the first day of the fall feast at this seventh month usually intend to signal the official end of the late crop's harvest. The *final* fall feast of Trumpets is considered the perfect time of Christ's second coming, not just a few months after the Rapture of the summer harvest, this time. No. Scripture is clear about the seven years of wrath that will happen before Christ's second coming. We know He will come on a feast day, and scripture declares He will come with trumpets blasting, and the host of heaven is coming with Him.

When Christ returns to mark the end to the seven-year tribulation, it will be for war and vengeance first and then to reap that final harvest of His chosen people.

He will glean the field and the four corners (Isaiah 11:12) left from the summer harvest, the Rapture. The Jews that rejected Him the first time He will reap as the final harvest.

Why will He gather them from the four corners of the earth? Understand that today, Israel has been scattered throughout the world. Only 30 percent of all the Jews live in Jerusalem. More Jews live in America than in Israel.

By the midpoint of the tribulation period, all the Jewish people will know that this is and always has been Jesus the Messiah, whom they pierced. They will acknowledge Him when He finally comes for them, and He will forgive them.

There will also be the remnant of those kind-of-believers who were not Raptured before the beginning of the tribulation. At this end of the tribulation, they will be sure believers now and will be accepted and forgiven as well.

Another section of Scripture, usually confused with the Rapture, is about the end-time harvest. This is made clear in the preliminary verses, saying, "as it was in the days of ..." Noah and Lot. The chosen are spared, and the wicked are destroyed. Verse 30 of Luke 17, says it will be this way when the "Son of Man is revealed." When He appears this final time, one (evil) will be taken (away) and the other left, to inherit the earth (Luke 17:26–37).

{Keith: Wheat, as it matures will bow its head.— Comment made after the parable of the wheat and the tares (weeds)}

> Matthew 13:24–30: (Christ said,) "Let both grow together until the harvest" (the harvest of His second coming). "I will say to the reapers, Gather ye together first the tares and and bind them in bundles to burn them, but gather the wheat into my barn."

Those trumpets will sound, and those already Raptured will be coming with Him and with a heavenly host of angels (Revelation 19:11–20:6). There will be a battle that won't last long.

> Revelation 19:19: "And I saw the beast, and the kings of the earth, and their armies gathered together to make war against Him that sat on the horse, and against His army. 20 And the beast was taken, and with him the false prophet that wrought miracles before him, with which he deceived them that had received the mark of the beast, and them that worshiped his image. These both were cast alive into a lake of fire burning with brimstone. 21 And the remnant were slain with the sword of Him that sat upon the horse, which sword proceeded out of His mouth (by His words) and all the fowls were filled with their flesh."

Next, Satan will be bound in chains under the earth for a thousand years.

> Revelation 20:1–2: "And I saw an angel come down from heaven, having the key to the bottomless pit and a great chain in his hand. 2 And he laid hold on the dragon, that old serpent, which is the Devil and Satan, and bound him a thousand years."

The rescued Jews and the Tribulation Saints who have endured will still be in human form and will repopulate the earth in this thousand-year period called the Millennial Reign.

With Satan chained below, there will be peace and joy with only Jesus among us. When that devil is released for a season, he will try the ones born during the Millennial Reign with temptations. Will this generation be wiser?

Soon, the battle of Armageddon will ensue. Do you wonder Who will win? (Read Revelation 20:7–10)

Considered the perfect day of the final Great White Throne Judgment, as spoken in Revelation 20:11–15, is the last Day of Atonement to end all judgment days.

The third fall feast is Tabernacles, which celebrates the freed Hebrew slaves living in tents in the desert of Arabia on their way to the land of promise.

When we celebrate this time, it will be our final home when we see New Jerusalem coming down from heaven. This occasion was described by John the Beloved as the disciple who laid his head on the chest of Jesus at their last meal, to whom Jesus gave the care of His mother from the cross. The same John who ran to the tomb with Peter that third morning writes his vision for us:

> Revelation 21:1–4: "And I saw a new heaven and a new earth: for the first heaven and the first earth were passed away, and there was no more sea. 2 And I, John, saw the holy city, new Jerusalem, coming down from God out of heaven, prepared as a bride adorned for

her husband. 3 And I heard a great voice out of heaven saying, Behold, the tabernacle of God is with men, and he will dwell with them, and they shall be his people and God Himself shall be with them, and be their God. 4 And God shall wipe away all tears from their eyes; and there shall be no more death, neither sorrow, nor crying, neither shall there be any more pain: for the former things are passed away."

Satan fell from heaven because of pride, wanting to exalt himself above God. Will pride be a threat in the New Heaven? Over breakfast at the local pancake place (7:30am Sunday, everyone welcome), Matt and Keith discussed this question and decided, no. There will not be pride in heaven this time. All of us will know we didn't earn the reward of heaven on our merit. We will be there only because we believed in Christ's blood sacrifice. It was His obedience that made the decision for all of us. His life alone is holy and sinless. He endured His personal hell of the absence of His Father on the cross until His work was finished. Glory! Glory to God in the Highest! Our faithful Lord and Savior, forever more! The Elders will cast their crowns at His feet and so will we. We will know the wonders of our eternity are because of Jesus.

Hope to see you there!